Women before God

Women before God

LAVINIA BYRNE

First published in Great Britain 1988
SPCK
Holy Trinity Church
Marylebone Road
London NW1 4DU

Second Impression 1989

British Library Cataloguing in Publication Data

Byrne, Lavinia
    Women before God.
    1. Women in Christianity
    I. Title
    262′.15 BV639.W7

    ISBN 0-281-04337-X

    Typeset by York House Typographic Ltd
    Printed in Great Britain by
    the Camelot Press, Southampton

To the memory of Ruth Morgan

Contents

Introduction

∾

The angel was sent by God . . . to a woman
LUKE 1.26-7

We live today in a world and a Church where women are speaking with a new voice and a new urgency. I have heard this voice in so many varied settings. The most public have been in conferences and seminars, in discussion groups and ·meetings. The most private have been in the context of one-to-one spiritual direction and retreat work and, above all, in conversation with my friends. I have heard it in a black women's refuge in Chicago; in an Ignatian retreat house in Ontario; read it in letters from Idaho and Massachusetts, Cambridge and Paris; seen it in family contexts in Middlesbrough and Hull. I have found it given immediacy in films and books, on the television and in the pulpit. I have heard it at prayer and I have met it at play. It is a voice which reminds me that I am made in God's image and likeness and that this is my glory.

I have been led to perceive that this voice is spoken from the place where Mary first heard the angel; the place of God's presence and purpose within. The Christian story began in this place, where God's angel can be sent to and received by a woman. Furthermore, Christbearing women have a wealth of insight and experience to bring to the present-day telling and interpretation of this story. We represent the positive side of the women's movement in both its Christian and its secular forms. I am aware, however, that while a great deal of feminist theology and of theology written by women has much to say about God, much to say about our current practice, about the position of women within the Church and our role in society, less of it speaks particularly clearly about our identity as believers and how we may grow as believers. My own purpose here is to look at the ways in which we bear Christ into the world and how we may nurture the divine life within ourselves and in others.

One persistent image from the Old Testament haunts my

memory, the image of mount Zion, the 'city of the great King' (Ps. 48.2). For centuries, the Roman Catholic tradition for one has taken this symbol of God's presence in the world and applied it to Mary as ideal woman and to the Church as ideal community. At present, however, the image is becoming diffused as more and more real women are discovering themselves as the 'citadel where God has shown himself a sure defence' (Ps. 48.3). I write this book because my understanding is that where women 'walk around Zion, go round about her, number her towers, consider well her ramparts, go through her citadels,' that is to say, where we come to self-awareness and self-knowledge, then indeed may we 'tell the next generation that this is God' (Ps. 48.12–13). For 'God is in the midst of her, she shall not be moved' (Ps. 46.5).

The individual disciple is committed to a journey in faith where movement will be from certainty to mystery. When I look at what has happened in my own life I find that I have been asked to abandon the absolutes of childhood in favour of the richness of news that is always good and always new. I have discovered faith to be different to certainty. For faith is about growth in the knowledge and love of God, whilst certainty is self-defining and self-justifying. Faith is a gift from the hand of a God who is always greater than anything we can say about God; certainty a possession. The one can be shared; the other can all too easily be hoarded. 'How do women become disciples?' is a specific question and one which is increasingly being asked. In any form of ministry to the spiritual development of women, images of holiness and ministry taken from the tradition must be re-examined. Are they a blueprint for women to follow or a minefield we must avoid? How do we grow in the knowledge and love of God? How do we pray? What are the insights we bring from 2000 years of invisibility and cast into the light? What is the certainty we come from, and the mystery into which we move?

In so far as women or feminist theologians are writing about God and the Church in new ways their thinking necessarily stimulates development in the area of Christian spirituality and feeds in answers to these questions. As a Roman Catholic I find that what is needed is the confidence to accept and listen both to the tradition and to these new voices; to own the prejudice and bias that result from a tradition which has denied that God can speak to individuals, especially – let it be said – if they are women. What is implied is that personal faith development is not the dangerous activity some have feared. My understanding is that the Church can only be alive to the extent that the women and men who form faith community together within it are alive; the Church finds God in their seeking and finding, a timeless God who nevertheless can speak to contemporary need, the God whose angel came to a woman.

I write as a Christian, as a woman, as a person who is grateful to the feminists for opening my eyes to certain issues and problems. More significantly I write as a Roman Catholic and as an apostolic religious sister; as a member of a Church and religious Order that have a particular heritage and style. I do not apologize for these, but likewise cannot ignore them, and would not expect what I think and feel and have to say to be universally valid and totally unconditioned. I write as someone who works in an Institute of Spirituality on the editorial staff of *The Way;* that is to say, as someone who is professionally engaged in spiritual direction and retreat work, in teaching and discussion, reading and writing about the way in which people grow as believers, and what it is we mean when we talk about faith formation and faith development. I write as a person who has been forced to admit that she has her own personal biases and prejudices and perceptions. Many of these are bits of mental furniture that need to be spring-cleaned or cleared to the attic or the skip, but many of them are increasingly fighting their way to a place of honour in my personal household, and becoming well-used and well-worn as I share them with other people.

I write for women – though not exclusively for women – who want to integrate their experience into the mainstream of the Church's life; women who believe, even in unreflected ways, that God is to be sought and found in all things; that they have the freedom to refer everything to God. I write for women who are trying to live present to God in ordinary, everyday situations and to meet God in relationships and within their own reactions to these situations and relationships; women whose personal faith is expressed in a growing response as they begin to be aware of God present in all things, absent from none; women who, when they go to church, want to bring this experience with them and celebrate it there.

The rest of this book explores ways in which each of us

personally, and women in particular, can grow in the knowledge and love of God, how personal faith can develop in today's Church and today's world. This present-day perspective is important because it enables questions raised by contemporary theology to inform any exploration. The first four chapters, therefore, ask how we experience ourselves as *belonging* – inside ourselves, inside our experience, inside our world and inside our Church. Any quest for meaning has a context. My own began in such safe and sheltered ways and is captured so hauntingly in the First Communion photograph I have taken to hanging up in my bedroom. In it I wear a long white dress, with a hanging pocket to carry a mother-of-pearl rosary. In fact I have the rosary in a white-gloved hand, and the photographer used the veil I wore to create an aura of soft white light around my head. My childish devotion was nurtured by a system of symbols and practices I may now have discarded but which are as familiar to me as the air I breathe, and which I no longer feel I have to try to interpret or understand. I grew up surrounded by candles and statues; I had a little altar set out in my bedroom and collected prayer books and holy pictures. Now I find that I can return to these and the symbols with which we have replaced them more selectively, and choose things old and new from my treasure house. By belonging to my own story and finding that it traces the pattern of my growth as a believing Christian woman, I find that God is the God who brings together every thread of my experience because it was she who first knit me into being. This God is not a God who drops stitches or despairs of her task.

The second half of the book develops some of these insights and takes the debate further. This means moving beyond a definition that would see discipleship in too narrow a context, beyond a sacred/secular divide, beyond the thinking behind our use of the expression 'having a vocation', and beyond questions raised by the movement to ordain women. It means looking at the development of our own personal spirituality, at how we pray, at the presence of Christian women in the world and in the Churches. The integrating spirituality which the text tries to explore looks both to the tradition and to the future of an increasingly whole and increasingly adult Church.

The book has some characteristics which require comment or explanation. I am reluctant to name God in ways which are gender specific; that is to say, I have avoided the pronouns 'he' or 'she' except where they have particular force and importance. Equally, I have chosen to write in a way that deliberately explores my theme: to return to certain ideas according to a spiral rather than a linear way of reflecting on them. Chapters one, two, three and four introduce questions that return in chapters five, six, seven and eight. If you wish to read the book in a linear way, read it as follows: one/five, two/six, three/seven, four/eight. I have deliberately avoided cluttering up the text with references and footnotes; a list of the principal works I have mentioned or quoted from is included in the bibliography.

Both during my own personal journey as a believing woman and during the writing of this book I have received the support of many friends. I trust that these friends will recognize their own voices in the text. My editor at SPCK, Judith Longman; Angela Tilby, the reader; David Lonsdale, Philip Sheldrake and Mary Critchley with whom I work; my own IBVM community in London, and those who have read the manuscript for me along the way, must receive personal thanks for their kindness and help.

Feast of the Transfiguration
6 August 1987

Part One

1
What are Women Saying?

Some women of our company say . . .

LUKE 24.22

Different or inferior?

Why do I find it so difficult to call myself a feminist? For a year I
have wrestled with this question and am only now coming to
recognize some kind of answer. Our world is necessarily a world of
differences, and so of tension. I can experience this tension in ways
that seem to threaten me and fill me with dread or I can look at it
with the eyes of faith. I saw this so clearly four years ago when I
preached at the memorial service of a friend who had died on
Maundy Thursday. I found myself saying , 'To die in Holy Week
is such a privilege and Maundy Thursday the more mysterious
day. In baptism Ruth took on the pattern of Christ's death and
resurrection, she undertook to make his way her own. His way
confounds our preconceptions, our frightening fear and mistrust,
for Jesus turned his face to Jerusalem, and made his way there
purposefully, knowing that failure is not about God's displeasure,
that success is not the same as salvation.'

While she was dying I spent quiet hours by her bed and had time
to reflect on what I was seeing there. Here was someone I loved and
admired, the best teacher I had had at university, someone whose
quest for excellence marked every single thing she undertook,
dying at the age of forty-two. I found myself asking her, 'It isn't
tragic, this death, is it?' and hearing her say, 'Oh no.' Not only had
she lived well but she died well, because she sought truth even in
this. I am writing for her here because I believe that she taught me
by example a great deal of what I am coming to understand now
about being a Christbearing woman in the world. She knew about
being strong and being weak, about sickness and health, about

3

being a woman rather than a man. She showed me that the way to live creatively with the tension of human differences is not to imagine that God loves one more than the other and so grasp at neither. She showed me that God may be sought and found in all things, because failure is not about God's displeasure and because it is so wrong to equate success with salvation.

Four years is a long time to spend deepening an understanding, and yet I have needed each of those years and will need more again to let what I saw then transform how I live now. For I catch myself seeking phoney solutions. And so, for example, I will pretend that I am poor rather than admit I am rich, which because I live in both the northern hemisphere and the Western world I inevitably am. I will pretend that I am no colour at all rather than acknowledge that I am white. I will be frightened by sickness and avoid the halt and the lame where I do not rejoice in my own good health. I have been intrigued to find that I pretend neutrality in the face of these differences – about being rich/poor, white/black, healthy/sick – although they appear to put me in a position that would make me feel advantaged, and even though they appear to be things which are beyond my control. One of the ways I do this is by denying these differences exist. Another is by seeking to resolve or over-come them. The third way, of living with them, is the most creative way, the way of valuing them as an insight into the vision of God.

Then I notice that I also resist other dualisms or differences, when, for example, I cannot get myself to use words such as 'woman' or 'sinner' or speak of 'my body' and 'my experience', which in fact mean something considerably more fundamental to me. When I end up denying that I am a woman and a sinner and that I have my own story and set of experiences, including those which go with being rich and white and healthy, my whole identity is in jeopardy. For in this way I deny God's gift of me to me, God's presence in the midst of me. And yet if I really am made in God's image and likeness I know that I am to seek God within them, myself within God. This is my glory.

Why do I find it so difficult to name myself with these words? One reason, I believe, is that the Christian Churches have made it difficult for me to use them in anything but hierarchical terms and so as part of a debate about grasping or power. For in the male/female, the saint/sinner or spirit/body dualisms I always come off a loser. Christian feminists have helped me understand this, and if I can now name myself as woman and sinner and as coming to God in my body and person and experience then I owe thanks to them and to the work they have done to make me – and so many other women – aware. Amongst other things they have made me more sensitive to the texts of the Church's tradition. They enable me to perceive that there is not just a valid difference (which is God-given and God-filled) but a sense of hierarchy and hence a put-down behind passages such as these:

> The husband . . . will always want his spouse to have a beautiful appearance and a beautiful figure, to move graciously and to dress elegantly; he will also be proud if she has read Shakespeare and Tolstoy, but he is also practical and likes to eat well so he will be doubly happy if he discovers that in addition to a beautiful spouse he has acquired a priceless queen of the kitchen and queen of the sparkling floors and of a house made beautiful by delicate hands and of children brought up as living flowers.
>
> (John Paul I, while still a cardinal)

> Let a woman learn in silence with all submissiveness. I permit no woman to teach or to have authority over men; she is to keep silent. For Adam was formed first, then Eve; and Adam was not deceived, but the woman was deceived and became a transgressor.
>
> (St Paul, 1 Tim. 2.11–14)

> In many countries a charter for women which would put an end to an actual discrimination and would establish relationships of equality in rights and of respect for their dignity is the object of study and at times of lively demands. We do not have in mind that false equality which would be in contradiction with woman's proper role . . .
>
> (Paul VI, *Octogesimo Adveniens*)

> Woman! You are the Devil's doorway. You have led astray one who the Devil would not dare attack directly. It is your fault that the Son of God had to die; you should always go in mourning and rags.
>
> (Tertullian)

5

Amongst all the savage beasts none is found so harmful as woman.

(John Chrysostom)

Woman is an occasional and incomplete being, a misbegotten male. It is unchangeable that woman is destined to live under man's influence and has no authority from her Lord.

(Thomas Aquinas)

Woman is a sick she-ass . . . a hideous tapeworm . . . the advance post of hell.

(John Damascene)

When I deprecate female suffrage I am pleading for the dignity of woman. I am contending for her honour, I am striving to perpetuate those peerless prerogatives inherent in her sex, those charms and graces which exalt womanhood and make her the ornament and coveted companion of man. Woman is queen indeed, but her empire is the domestic kingdom.

(Cardinal Gibbons of Baltimore)

The image of God is found in the man, not the woman, for man is the beginning and end of woman.

(Thomas Aquinas)

Each of these texts tells me not just that I am different, but that I am inferior. The assumption behind each of them is that women are inferior to men. A 'natural order' is presupposed, where women are hopelessly sentimentalized as 'queen indeed' and then dismissed, where our influence is spelt out in terms of a 'proper role'. Our empire is to be a domestic one; we are destined to live *under* man's influence, to be man's ornament and coveted companion, to be lesser beings. That is why such texts are shocking and so painful to live with; that is why living in a sexist Church is so painful. We know that we have to accept the fundamental truth presented by the other polarities – about being rich or poor, black or white, well or sick. They only hold hidden dangers when we deny them or assume that God is attracted to one and not to the other. Yet Jesus loved both rich and poor. We know, too, that colour prejudice is tied to fear and not to love, that the mechanism of projection is the most pernicious of all because ultimately we are redeemed only when we accept whatever it is we fear. We know that God may be sought and found in weakness and sickness as well as in strength and in health. The differences or polarities are there and have their own validity. They challenge us to accept all these opposites and all that God is offering us in these opposites. They challenge us to accept what we really know, that God loves unselectively and is not concerned to say that to be one is better than to be the other. God is already present within the opposites; to reject either is to reject God and to limit our access to God, God's to us.

I believe that the problem for women is that the Christian tradition has been less open to human differences than the Gospels are; the tradition has thought it necessary to set up one half of the human family at the expense of the other. It has presented us with an ascendant white, male, celibate priesthood and put the control of Church teaching into their hands. One consequence is that, as women, we have been forced to *define* our identity in ways that lead us to *deny* that identity. Hence, too, my misgivings with feminism, because it seems to buy into the same denials. The Christian feminist is apparently being asked to change, to become something different again, as though to be woman is not good enough. Behind this there seems to me to be a denial of the fact that God loves women for a very simple reason. God looks on us with the total love of recognition, God knows us from within because God is within. The Christian feminist is somehow being asked to change, to read 'woman' as a dirty word and to opt out of the tension that comes from being part of a dualism. Thereby she is in effect choosing to perpetuate the system that reads dualisms as a power structure or hierarchy rather than as a gift of God and a challenge to our limiting ways of thinking.

Right now, in fact, I find myself seeking another way of using the tension that comes from living within the male/female polarity. The solution, for me, is not to become this third category, a feminist, but to opt to live as Christian woman as fully as possible. Only in this way can the other dualisms be explored as I begin to learn that God is at work in my life and all my experience. My task becomes to say 'Yes, it is good being a woman, a sinner, within my body, as a rich, healthy Western European.' Only in this can I experience that God is not prepared to name male as superior to female and to learn to find God also when I am poor and sick and fearful.

What I am suggesting is that the Christbearing woman is asked to accept that God already loves her as woman, that God desires only that she accept this identity and so receive her power from within. The Christbearing woman is asked to free both herself and other Christians – notably men – from false images of human development. She does not enter a polemic where some become oppressed and some oppressors. She seeks the truth that lies within; the truth that to be woman is good and God-filled and God-assured. She is asked to explore what it means to be made in God's image and likeness, to claim this profound truth about herself and give it a public face in God's world.

My own journey to this insight has been a lonely one and yet not one I have conducted alone. I am very fortunate. I entered a convent at the age of seventeen. What I am saying is that from the age of seventeen, or maybe from the age of fourteen when this desire first began to grow in me, I have been searching for God in the company of other women. Only over the last five years has this search had political overtones; only over the last five years have I allowed myself to feel the pain of being a woman in the Roman Catholic communion; only over the last five years have I begun to search for God within this experience.

For this reason too, because I am becoming aware of the freedom I enjoy as a woman to find God now, here, I am reluctant to take on board elements of any separatist theology, whether that of women or of men, and the inferences that can be drawn from it. I believe that feminism has raised the right questions; I am not certain about some of its answers. What is at issue is not something about power, or power-sharing, or women claiming their rights, but something to do with the celebration of the identity and experience of believing women; something about what happens when a woman says 'I believe' and finds that God empowers her from within; that God is speaking in her ability to say 'I' as well as being the one in whom she is proclaiming belief.

I am gradually learning that experience is to be celebrated because within human experience the meeting with God has already taken place. Within this experience God is already at work and known by name. Where any woman says 'I know and love you' to God or to another human being, something distinctive is being said, and that is what I am anxious to explore. I am convinced that God will be freed and God's voice will be heard in quite new ways when this knowing and loving are allowed to inform the Church's teaching and practice. If the sense of newness and purpose that have come from the rise of feminism are to be fed into the Church's mainstream life, however, then it has to be when women are free to say it is good to be women and it is bad to oppress women in the name of anything. What is called for is a radically new way of looking at the position of women before God; a radically new way of attending to the voice of believing women.

Naming ourselves before God

How have I come to hear this particular call? I suppose that the debate about using words in church that exclude or include women has forced me to ask what is happening when I am not named there, and so – in this formal context at any rate – deprived of the use of speech. What is good language and what is bad language in any church context? Good language is language that communicates well, either in the restricted code used in our domestic setting or in the wider code used in our 'public lives'. Bad language is language that fails to communicate, fails to allow us to speak of what we know, fails to speak to us significantly. And because language is so powerful, the way in which we use it either to include or to exclude other people is far more important than we ordinarily admit. Bad language denies one of the most basic of human rights, the right to existence, the right to take our place as members of the domestic or the public group. Bad language denies us our place within the noun or pronoun governing the verbs used to communicate this experience of belonging. It blocks out both who we are and what we do. The Church's bad language inhibits us when we seek to name ourselves before God. It makes a difference not simply to our theology or the way in which we think about God but also to our spirituality, the way in which we live and pray in terms of what we believe. It institutionalizes hierarchical thinking and this bedevils the way God asks us to live with the variety of being women and men.

And so the language we use in church is critical to our identity as people who are to say 'I believe' or 'we believe'. How the Church is to appear before God as a grace-filled, faith-filled community is dependent upon the way in which as believers we are free to name ourselves and our experience. If discipleship is about seeking and finding God in every event and relationship, then I must be able to name this in church. As a believer I need to be able to name myself as someone who is looking for God both within the community of believers on a Sunday and within my everyday situation and everyday contacts, because I am the same person when I go to church as I am when I make Church in the community of my own home or neighbourhood. Discipleship is not going to take me away from either of these.

When the language offered for our use in church fails to name women it excludes me and most of what I do. It allows me neither to celebrate my own identity nor to reflect upon the place of God in my experience. On reflection I now see that the inferences of this for women believers are far more significant than I first realized. The presence of women in the community of the faithful is denied by the prayers used in formal liturgical contexts. The service of women in the community of the faithful, and notably in the base community of our own domestic setting, is denied by coupling those particular nouns, pronouns and verbs. The faith development of women is undermined where the saving action of God is appropriated by half the human race and not the other half. The personal faith response of praying women cannot but be influenced by sexism, however hard we try to resist this. Our faith development and our prayer, our presence in the world as believers and our service in God's Church are so fundamental a part of any form of Christian discipleship that the balance has somehow to be redressed. This ultimately is what I mean when I say that the dualism should remain but must be redeemed. Men and women *are* different. What has to go is the claim that either one is superior to the other.

Increasingly I have been forced to ask, why should our identity be concealed? One day, in a London restaurant, I found myself weeping while having supper with three men whom I love dearly, as they discussed whether or not women should be ordained. I found myself asking this question, 'What have I done wrong?' The only women who do 'make it' to collects and prefaces seem to be examples or role models representing certain notions held by men rather than familiar people whose experience of trying to come to God in the real world is held up for my encouragement. Increasingly I have found myself in the trap set up by the antithesis 'queen' and 'shining floors', 'queen' and 'domestic empire'. This does nothing to help women for whom home is indeed the place where they seek and find God, and nothing for women who work out of the home. The woman who is both virgin and mother, or queen and nun, or child and martyr is such a very difficult act to follow. She has been removed from the tension of the real polarity within which I am asked to find my identity, the polarity of being woman rather than man, and has been set apart in some artificial construct which represents a false dilemma.

The women I know and with whom I have worked as a spiritual director and retreat director are women who proclaim God's greatness, whose spirit rejoices in God; women who stand, who pray and who remember; women whose lives shape the human family, who ask for the power to love, to feel and to heal. They are naming ways in which we are all seeking to grow as believers and yet their voice has a very specific accent. I listen to it with great care because I believe that I can hear the sound of God's voice in what they are saying to me. There are women in our company who are increasingly saying what I read in a letter from a friend: 'My self rests in God; the journey to find self is, I think, coming to an end' (letter from Barbara Harrison, 15 June 1987).

I have found that since I have 'given myself permission' to reflect on the prayers I hear in church and match them against what happens when I pray alone or when I listen to these women, the way in which the voice of believing women has been silenced becomes even more apparent. Moreover the discrepancy is much more obvious when I look at the verbs than when I look at the nouns.

If the community of the faithful is communicating its deepest insights in the language we use when at prayer, then the feminists are right. The news for women is bad rather than good. For this reason, too, many women, and religious sisters in particular, find it increasingly difficult to pray the Divine Office as set out in the Roman breviary. The formal language of the breviary, and especially of the prayers of intercession, no longer makes sense. The activities suggested there as ways of helping the Kingdom of God grow within seem to rely upon images of strife and of construction engineering, and imply that the Kingdom is about numbers and noise rather than attitudes and values. The effect of hearing the Church at prayer distances me and other women I know because we can no longer identify with the sentiments that are being attributed to us. An effect of this is to make us question the

Church's relevance to and interest in whatever else is important to us. Where the Church prevents us from speaking, it no longer speaks to us. The silence is becoming mutual. For inclusive language to work, it has to be taken to its logical conclusion. Words like 'hold', 'enfold', 'touch', 'embrace' must appear alongside words like 'build', 'strike', 'fill' and 'complete'; the imagery of creation must be fed into that of destruction. For both what we are and what we do are there to be celebrated.

This bias and the way in which it necessarily affects the way we pray is not shared by the Bible to quite the same extent. Women are named there and our stories appear alongside the stories of men. Even where these are short or are concealed in the text, they can still be used by women at prayer. In the context of retreat work, I have noticed that women find themselves praying in quite unexpected ways when given texts from those parts of the Bible such as the Song of Songs or the stories of Deborah or Judith or Ruth, for instance, in which we are named and our experience is demonstrated to be the arena of God's activity in the world. There are so many different Magnificats within the Scripture texts and within the hearts of each of us, and these cry out to be released. Beyond these songs of liberation there are other psalms where the gestures of the visitation scene in Luke's Gospel are repeated. The child we all bear as herald of God's coming can leap for joy at every recognition of this coming; our love can be echoed in every wind and spoken in every star.

The Gospel has hidden and missing figures as well; such as the mother of the prodigal son, the women who stayed at home while their husbands minded sheep by night or gazed at a star. 'The wise man finds, weeping in a crib him whom he sought for shining in the stars' (St Peter Chrysologus, Sermon 160). The wise woman meanwhile has already had to find what she seeks in the child she bears within, in the child she bears and cradles and nurtures into the world. It was my mother who told me that she had a lot of sympathy for the shepherds' wives because they had to get on with the cooking. When I pray with these women I get a deeper insight into the Christian story and its place in my life. Even the Gospel women who are kaleidoscoped into single characters and given generic names like Mary help me to find the threads and strands of my own complicated self more easily. Above all they help me identify the way in which God seems to treat and to value women, as reflected in the way Jesus relates to women. The psalms, too, are a gold-mine because the images they use, such as that of mount Zion with which I began, can be reappropriated and feed God's life within the Christbearing woman. Each of us is a tower of ivory, house of gold and ark of the covenant. Each of us is a morning star. These are images which, in the Roman Catholic tradition at least, used to be restricted by being applied only to Mary. As a young nun I said the Litany of Loreto daily and gazed at stained glass windows where the titles it uses were set out pictorially. Only recently has it dawned on me that they are true of every woman. I am learning what Uzziah saw in Judith, that 'from the beginning of your life all the people have recognized your understanding, for your heart's disposition is right' (Judith 8.29). My friend is right: 'The journey to find self is, I think, coming to an end.'

Naming God

For who is the God in whom we seek to believe? The one named by the Christian tradition in purely patriarchal terms, or the God of mystery who is stirring so strongly in the Churches at present? What happens when we both name and pray to God in new ways? Just as the identity and experience of half the human race are denied when we fail to name women in the language we use in church, so, and more importantly, we fail to name and know the God in whose image we are made when we only call him Father, Son and Spirit. God the sustainer, God the redeemer and God the sanctifier present models of wholeness to us in which we can all – both women and men – seek and find our innermost selves. Similarly, where God is named as Source of all Being, Eternal Word and Holy Spirit, we are free to image him – or her – in fresh ways. Moreover, if we feel we need permission to name God in these ways, we have only to look at the Scriptures to find that there the power to name is itself cherished more than some of the names we in fact use.

So God who is rock (Ps. 144.1) and mighty stronghold (Ps. 144.2) is also shepherd (Ps. 23.1) and beloved (Song of Songs 2.8). God who is vinedresser (John 15.1) and master of the vineyard (Matt. 21.33) is also mother hen clucking over her brood (Matt. 23.37). God who is mighty warrior (Ps. 136.18) is also spirit hovering over the waters (Gen. 1.2) and playing in the world (Prov. 8.31). God is light and truth and way (John 14.6), as well as person and mystery. Where the promise was that the Lord would bare his holy arm (Isa. 52.10), he is in fact revealed as child laid in a manger (Luke 2.7). God acted out in verbs is a God who watches over, loves, draws out, embraces, touches, heals, feeds the people. God may be pillar of fire by night but this God is cloud by day. God is comfort and solace of the people.

Other texts hidden in the Church's tradition speak in the same maternal language. At times the imagery is almost overwhelming:

> A cup of milk was offered to me, And I drank it in the sweetness of the Lord's kindness. The Son is the cup, And the Father is He who is milked; And the Holy Spirit is She who milked Him; Because His breasts were full, And it was undesirable that His milk should be ineffectually released. The Holy Spirit opened Her bosom, And mixed the milk of the two breasts of the Father.

In this passage from the *Odes of Solomon*, a collection of Syriac texts which their present-day editor has called the 'earliest Christian hymn-book', both the Spirit and the Father are mother feeding the Son, and the Christian is offered milk from the same cup, asked to partake of the same understanding. For if God is described in certain ways in texts such as these, an invitation is implied; the reader, too, can grow into a similar understanding. To name God newly is not enough. We have also to pray to God newly named; to drink where 'the people were very thirsty' (Judith 8.30). Even the more familiar passages from, for example, the writings of Julian of Norwich are in a sense offering us a similar choice:

> This fair lovely word 'mother' is so sweet and so kind in itself that it cannot truly be said of anyone or to anyone except of him and to him who is the true Mother of life and of all things. To the property of motherhood belong nature, love, wisdom and knowledge, and this is God. For though it may be so that our bodily bringing to birth is only little, humble and simple in comparison with our spiritual bringing to birth, still it is he who does it in the creatures by whom it is done. The kind, loving mother who knows and sees the need of her child guards it very tenderly, as the nature and condition of motherhood will have.
>
> *Showings* Long text, ch. 60

And less familiar words, like those of Mary Ward, the seventeenth-century Englishwoman who founded the first community of religious women to be without traditional monastic structures, are spoken with equal freedom: 'O Parent of parents and Friend of all friends, without entreaty thou tookest me and led me from all else that at length I might see and settle my love in thee.'

Once again both nouns and verbs communicate something of the flavour of how these women perceived God. God who knows, sees and guards, God who takes and leads is described effortlessly in language that depends on maternal imagery or the imagery of familiar human relationships. Texts such as these presuppose that all the language we use to describe God is analogous, that we are bound to rely upon familiar categories when we speak of the God of mystery. Every name we use is partial, even the most hallowed names from the tradition; we need them all, and other fresh names, in order to begin to speak. Jesus was prepared to use a new name such as this when he called God 'Father' or 'Abba'. In doing this he was naming God certainly, but also naming himself as Son. With every name we use we are also describing ourselves and the relationship that exists between ourselves and God.

For this reason, when we allow ourselves to pray to a God who is imaged as mother as well as father, as woman as well as man, we are able to find our own identity within God, God within our own identity. This gives quite a new base from which to live with the variety of being woman as opposed to being man, one which is about being very good in God's eyes. As a young woman of twenty-four Mary Ward looked in a mirror while she combed her hair and found herself repeating the words 'Glory, glory, glory'. The God who is mystery is within the midst of us, within us, within me. I have to go no further.

Where God is newly imaged like this and named as mother or parent or friend, where the experience of praying women is allowed to speak authoritatively, then I am hearing something about my human identity as woman before God just as much as we all are about the God who made us male and female. In prayer we name both our relationship with God and the relationship we enjoy or fail to enjoy with each other. For this reason the freedom women have to use inclusive language in their ordinary, everyday domestic or public lives must be extended to how we are allowed to speak and what we are allowed to say in church; that is to say within the community of believers. With words we name both ourselves and God and begin to explore the relationship that exists between us. We name the ecclesial community as a whole community or as a fragmented community, for the pronoun 'we' embraces the dualisms within every divide: between priest and people, between women and men, between old and young. The pronoun 'we' acknowledges that there are differences but prevents them from becoming hierarchies. It does not provide an escape route from the questions which feminism raises but it could be that it commits us all – both women and men – to face and answer them.

God, too, is freed once named less exclusively in patriarchal categories, and the woman believer is able to explore herself within God, God within herself, and to grow in this understanding. With this in mind, chapter five will examine patterns of faith development as they affect the self-identity of believing, praying women and see what happens when women and God are named in new ways. For beyond the naming of God either as mother or as father there remains the God of mystery and the mystery of our own being. 'The journey to find God is, I think, coming to an end.'

2
What are Women Doing?

∽

The women went to the tomb with the spices they had prepared
LUKE 24.1

Being, doing – and having

Beyond the question of language – which highlights who I am –
there is another question raised by feminists which also continues
to preoccupy me, namely that of sexual stereotyping. This highlights what I do. There are times when we can all be cast into roles
and our identity seems to be both programmed and limited by the
experience we are allowed to have. Certain unexamined customs
and traditions can be the expression of values and principles in
which we do not believe, and yet they appear to dictate the script
for much of our day-to-day living. What we are allowed to do
appears to dictate who we are allowed to be, rather than to express
who we are. Any one of us can end up being allowed to anoint a
dead Jesus because this is the custom, while we are not allowed to
touch the living one who is with us all the time. Moreover,
anointing – of the sick for instance, with holy oils – is 'all right'
because it so clearly belongs to the vocabulary of religious experience and expression. The straightforward touching we do daily is
less all right. It has been separated away from the domain of the
religious, has been secularized and somehow 'magicalized' as
though it were toxic and to be put outside the sanctuary.

Where the feminists challenge the thinking behind sexual
stereotyping they highlight the connections between being and
doing. They argue that women should not have their access to
certain levels of human activity curtailed by social or emotional
convention. So far so good, but I think the believer has to take the
debate further and look for more clarification, because this is a
question about faith and not just about power. By this I mean that

17

what is at issue is not simply women's access to more activities but our relationship to our own experience. What matters to me is not whether I can be a lorry driver but whether I can seek and find God in what I already do, God at work in the mystery of my being and doing. If within my present experience I then hear a call to be a lorry driver, I will go ahead and drive lorries – whatever the consequences. To operate this way round is very freeing. It means that I am committed both to celebrating who I am and what I do as woman before God and to listening attentively to the call of God within my everyday life.

There are certain scripts which are less helpful than this. I have found that the ones which are most harmful to women are those which value having before they value being and doing. Even where this has been seen as a new method of examining the relationship between identity and experience, the basic premise has been that having is good as it empowers. This stands in flat contradiction to the radical way in which the gospel would have us see human relationships transformed, for there it is loving that empowers, not having.

Gospel power is heady stuff and ambiguous in the way it operates; love is not meek and mild but tough and inventive. The power of which Mary speaks in her Magnificat is going to over-throw strong people: the proud, the mighty, the rich. None of them will be able to resist this power because its basis is something to do with God and God's resources rather than with the externals we associate with control. Those who trust only in their own strength will lose control. Those who are brought to their knees meanwhile, and who learn not to trust in their own resourceful-ness, are not doomed to stay there for ever. Rather, they can be transformed or raised up, freed to live out of a different set of values and understandings. Both doing and being are valued where the God who is love, and who empowers our loving, is our saviour. This is more than God the liberator; this is the God who enables us to see the child who is Jesus actively present within the Christbearing woman.

And so I am drawn to look at life and relationships as a place where this saving God is already at work, because I am confident that women are empowered thereby. That is to say we are reminded of the access we already enjoy to a God who loves us into life, and who values us as praying women. If I sound both happy and upset as I do this, should I feel ashamed? Where does this energy come from and what does it lead me to? I have had to spend time looking at my sense of disappointment and unease, have had to mourn the passing of my earlier certainties and the uncomplicated life they allowed me to live. I have noticed how easy it is to become depressed in order to avoid feeling angry. Somehow, however, I have found the energy to say what my real experience as a Roman Catholic woman is, to say what it feels like being excluded from the processes whereby I may celebrate this, or share in the way my Church makes decisions, or even the way in which it names God.

I have been led to reflect on the place of God in my life and relationships and this, more than anything else, has led me to stop dodging the issues that are in question. To write a book such as this may not be to become a lorry driver but it represents a comparable venture. It represents a way of celebrating the God who is at work in the world of everyday things and so of coming to live and pray within the world of everyday things.

God at work in my life

The God who is at work within my life is a God who leads me to look reflectively at the ways in which I experience myself as a believer in a given context. This context, in my own case, is made like an onion. All of it is me, yet it has many layers, some closer to my innermost centre, some less so. If any of these layers becomes my enemy, that is to say if it begins to form into a false brown shell and so to impede my growth, then I have to peel it away, however dearly I love it and would prefer to remain within its security. My context has a history; it is made up of my family, my childhood and schooling, my discovery of the world about me, my journey as a person consecrated by vows of poverty, chastity and obedience in a specific religious institute, the various places in which I work and have worked, the people I have known and loved. My context has a Church face as well; I was a pious child and am a practising adult.

If I am to come to God as I am, then I have firstly to get to know my context in all its complexity, and secondly to befriend it. I have to look inside the onion and observe that it is not as nice and regular as I perhaps thought. I would love each layer to be a perfect shell. I would love to find nothing but sweetness and light within. The reality is a little different, and peeling onions is never a particularly cheerful task. Until I do this work, however, I will inevitably live on the surface of my experience and be forced to look for a certain kind of God, one who is 'out there' and disengaged. Whatever I read in the Bible about God's love and care for me, whatever I hear in church about God's desire to intervene in my life, will be contradicted by my fears and dread of a God whom I secretly believe to be standing in judgement over me. All my fear of what might be concealed within me is used to turn God into a monster.

Once I embarked upon this work of looking at my own story as a place where God is coming to meet me, three things happened. First, my own version of the monster God was unmasked. I began to realize that I had been seeing God as a sledge-hammer, poised to crush my hands as I eased myself up from between the floorboards where I felt I belonged, and where I was increasingly unhappy. The second thing was that, for the first time in my life, I became actively conscious that I am a woman and that whole areas of my growth as a believing and praying person were being neglected where I failed to live as such. Third, this in turn meant re-imaging God, and so I was led to other pictures and understandings of a God who cradled me and loved me into life. Gradually, and reluctantly – because I hate controversy as much as anyone else – I was forced to look at what my Church made of my experience and what I might do about this. My perspective was sometimes a power perspective and sometimes a faith perspective; sometimes something between the two. If I am now attempting to integrate my identity and experience, this is because I am convinced that the call of God will be heard more clearly by someone who makes friends with her own process.

God at work in my relationships

Making friends with oneself means allowing other people to come close as well. Some of the work I have done and seen done, notably by other religious sisters, has been in the area of faith sharing, the healing of memories and the search for some kind of life map. A useful exercise is to mark off the left-hand side of a large piece of paper into decades and then to fill in columns labelled: significant experiences, significant relationships, images of God, prayer styles, conversions, feelings. This can be done with words but most usefully it should be done in drawings or using colours. Then it becomes possible to see patterns in the way in which we have sought for meaning. The exercise is valuable because it enables these patterns to emerge and to be interpreted. There may have been times in my life when I thought that God was not interested in my experience; times in my life when I refused to let myself be empowered by the love of God and rested in false security. The principal pattern is of God's fidelity and constant call made known to me in the gift into my life of people who have been with me on the way.

The resilience of the human spirit to harmful messages is vindicated over and over again when people do an exercise such as this. I can capture an instance of these messages in words my mother used to quote from the nuns at the convent where she was at school. The children there were told, 'Where two are together, the devil's between,' yet they went out and made friends with each other; they chose each other as godparents when they in turn had children. Ironically, that convent is now closed. It ran out of nuns. The women who survived – and others like them – listened to their experience, noted what was life-enhancing and what killed, and acted out of what they discovered. This insight into the importance of love and friendship is a theological landmark for many people. It enables them, often for the first time, to question where God is and where God's Kingdom is. Married people and single people can do the exercise equally usefully because, ordinarily, the rich variety of all relationships suddenly has some kind of focus. What matters is not whether I am married, but whether or not I am a loving person. The essence of what I am about is revealed when I begin to look at its expression in my own story.

Making Church

To know is not enough. If the Gospel is to speak to our story and empower us, there is further work to be done. I have indicated that, as a believing and practising Christian, my life has a double context: that of my personal experience and that of the world in which I live, the place where my story meets the rest of the human story, the place where I make Church.

If I choose to examine this public context next, this is because I have to know and name it too. The two possible approaches remain, however. Either I can come as someone seeking power, wanting to extend the range of women's activities, or as someone who wants to find and celebrate her own experience. Either I can come as someone who reads variety and differences in hierarchical terms or as someone who is concerned to find God in the variety that comes from being woman rather than man. Within this second perspective I have then to try to claim and befriend my experience as a believing woman in a believing community. I do not undertake this task lightly, but am beginning to see that I do not undertake it alone. There are many women asking the same questions that I ask, and they too are hearing a call from God within their own experience.

The God who asks me to look at my own story and to notice the importance of my life and friends is a God who asks me to live out the Christian story too. God calls me and attracts me to believe and to belong. There is a promise and an invitation here, and the one is meaningless without the other. For this reason I have to turn again to what the Gospels say to me about the way in which Christians believe and belong to God and to each other.

To own and reclaim my place in the Christian story is to be forced to take seriously what the Gospels say about re-imaging power. Otherwise we remain stuck inside our own bad experience and are doomed to keep re-running the tapes of sexual politics. I have been dismayed to see how easy this is to do; how easy it is to remain trapped inside questions that become a kind of vortex. Solidarity with the oppressed is all very well, but not if it continues to cast some as oppressors. Now I see not just why Jesus preferred the poor but *how* he preferred them. He dwelt in their midst and thereby made the rich sufficiently uncomfortable for them to desire to change. He relativized our entire way of looking at what makes us rich and what makes us poor because 'he, who was divine, did not cling to his divinity' (Phil. 2.6).

The questions into which women can get trapped when playing the tapes of oppression appear under the guise of good. They sound all right and perhaps are necessary because initially they enable us to own our sense of alienation. Typically they run as follows: 'Are women closer to a gospel understanding of power than men?' The reasons would not be essential, they are not based in the difference – whether biological or emotional, imagined or real – between women and men, rather they are a result of the conditioning that most women have received. They reflect the cultural setting in which most of us have grown to adulthood. Of course many women have been treated as though inferior – even where we have claimed that ours is a secret power over, for instance, the purse or the heart strings. Of course most women have been patronized – allowed to be honorary men when it suited the prevailing establishment to confer this dignity upon us. Most women have been exploited, either emotionally, or sexually or domestically. Roles and attitudes have been attributed to us by men who wanted to remain in control. And where these role definitions controlled what women could do, they necessarily influenced what women could be and left men safely in charge of all the having, which was depicted as the sole resource for fully developed human life.

Yet nowadays we live in enlightened times. Feminists have written about sexual stereotyping and its effects; various myths have been exposed; various ghosts laid. We may live with the heritage of centuries of received attitudes but we are at last free to do something with them. And so I find myself asking, 'How can we all take more seriously what the gospel is saying about that other power, the power of love? Whom we should trust and why?'

This movement from alienation into love is available to everyone, for God the liberator is also God the giver who loves us into life. God alone can free us from romantic ideas or manipulative behaviour based on ill-considered roles we adopt or stereotypes we impose because we fail to love. This is true liberation because it sets us free.

I am always amazed by the predominant visual images put before the congregation in any Roman Catholic church. Mary the mother of Jesus is elevated on a plinth, she holds the child in her arms, has the sun and moon under her feet and is crowned and bedecked. Jesus himself, meanwhile, is stripped and naked, the man who hangs in agony on a cross. The actual experience of many of the women and men in the congregation just does not mirror what is depicted there. The more bejewelled the Virgin, the more the roles of the congregation are likely to be reversed in reality. Our icons in church are extraordinarily powerful. They both express our myths and give them shape and form. They reflect the hidden role-models which perpetuate what is in effect an oppressive system. They mask the reality of a hierarchical system by appearing to reverse it. When we start moving away from stereotyping human behaviour the myths behind our role-models have to be uncovered and re-examined.

Beyond the myths

What have the Churches done to free women from mistaken roles and attitudes, to take us down from a plinth without immediately nailing us on a cross? What have the Churches done to help those men who wanted to act justly and walk humbly with regard to women? What is being assumed when the only expression available to describe the relationship we all enjoy with God is called 'sonship'? I may be a 'daughter of God' but the words lie uncomfortably upon my lips because for years I have heard the words 'sons of God' used by my tradition or Church. The only variant, 'children of God', is even less helpful because it does not speak to my adult understanding. When any adult believer is asked, 'Who are you?', the range of answers made available for everyday use is small. Essentially, I suppose, I am a baptized person. Furthermore I am a religious, consecrated by vows of poverty, chastity and obedience. If I were married, but particularly if I were a single person, I would find that question even more difficult to answer. A definition in terms of relationships would give me something like, 'I am a son, well, daughter really, of God,' or 'I am a member of Father X's parish.' As for a description of what I do in the Church . . . Most of us would find that an awkward question to answer because everything we in fact do is apparently trivial and unimportant in religious terms. Only things like taking the collection or reading on Sunday or being on the parish council or the flower-arranging rota seem to matter. My own experience of trying to come to God in everyday ways and in my ordinary working life is discounted.

The tradition places certain models before me which leave me feeling even less comfortable. So many of them fail to speak to my condition because they glorify images of what it is to be a woman that are no longer credible. If I look at the women my own Church has chosen to canonize and the reasons why they have been presented to me as models I come up with facts and statistics that leave me cold. What is being sanctified when virgins and martyrs are honoured and married women are not? What are we saying about God when we find God's image exclusively in queens and nuns rather than in ordinary people?

What are Women Doing?

Recent studies of the sociological factors determining canonization give some interesting data: only in this century has the proportion of women to be canonized gone over twenty per cent (the canon of the Russian saints has less than a dozen women in it). One author asks, 'Does this mean that the cults of saints were a means by which a certain social order was legitimized or sacralized?' Does it indeed? Another asks us to consider that 'of 151 female saints fully 25, or one in six, suffered debilitating illness for much of their lives after conversion, while of 713 male saints only 22 were chronically ill'. Why? Because:

> Penitence and austerity were forms of religious expression easily accessible to women who aspired to holiness. They were among the regular features of the cloistered life, and they reinforced rather than challenged the medieval view of what was appropriate to the female sex. Vanity, lust and frivolity were regarded as the besetting sins of femininity; they could best be expiated by practices that banished pride, chastised the flesh, and disciplined the spirit.
>
> Donald Weinstein and Rudolf Bell
> *Saints and Society*, University of Chicago Press 1982

Neither of the two authors in question is a woman; both have isolated features that have already been noticed. Firstly, that the Church has been slow to give the lead and has copied the expectations society has of women rather than pioneering better ones, based on a valuing of the human in all its forms. The Church has imitated the world in describing women according to sexual stereotypes – nice girl, good wife, queen of the shining floors. Secondly, that women are thereby exploited emotionally, to banish pride; sexually, to chastise the flesh; and domestically, to discipline the spirit. What is it saying to believing people and what does it tell them about God?

For a start, such thinking does nothing to free men from the prevailing order; it merely reinforces the world-view that women are there to be used, that we are part of the package of possessions to which men have a right in virtue of their sex. As a child I remember seeing a wonderful woman in the ladies' lavatory in Nice where she was the attendant. She had set out a table in front of her with a white cloth, silver and glasses and was preparing to eat lobster. In this particular sanctuary at least she could treat herself to some ceremony and style. In this context she was not a possession. Where what we do whether we like it or not, is picked up as a statement of our public worth, women can become the ultimate possession and thereby beholden to men for our very existence. This is news we would rather not meet in church. After all we go there to be led forwards not backwards.

Believing people are women and men who are prepared to ask questions, we are committed to reflecting upon our own experience, and there is every reason for the Church to speak to our everyday concerns. Moreover, it could be argued that our interest is a sign of life, a sign that the Church is not 'they', someone out there; the Church is 'we', 'us', the community of the faithful, grouped around the word and the table at every word and every table. We sacramentalize where we make certain tables divine, and magicalize by making others mortal. Over and above this we introduce a toxic element by reserving the divine to men and the mortal to women. In this we act without faith.

Where people look to their Churches to do all their thinking for them, however, they are likely to receive their images of what it is to be human in ways that do a disservice to their own inner wisdom or self-understanding. Where people think that what happens at home and in their 'private' lives has nothing to do with religion, the sacred and the secular cannot meet. The hidden messages about the place of women and the place of men within the Christian story serve only to make us back off even further. And so most of us avoid reflecting on our own experience, less because the process is too painful and much more because we are being prevented from seeing this reflection as part of the way in which we may communicate with God and God with us. We conceive of prayer in a restricted way as though it meant saying prayers rather than a way of being with God in all that we are and do.

Reflection and the experience of God

This raises questions about how we experience God in any case. So great is the hold of church and sacrament and word on the popular imagination that we find it difficult to imagine that God communicates with us anywhere else. The 'real' presence is that presence assured by Jesus when he spoke of 'two or three gathered in my name, and there am I in the midst of them' (Matt. 18.20). What better way of describing the average Christian family, the average

Christian community? Yet when we fail to seek and find God wherever God is present and communicating with us, we inevitably put gold edges around this presence and doom him to dwell in church. The Old Testament tradition is ignored when we no longer look at reality with the eyes of faith as the Jews did, and start localizing God's presence, dividing our world by a false dualism into the 'sacred' and the 'secular'. What Jesus had to say in the New Testament, both in the Gospels and in the early burgeoning of the Church, is somehow irrelevant when we start worshipping on one particular mountain and then upon another rather than 'in spirit and in truth'; when we are not conscious of each other and of our own selves as 'real presence'.

A problem could be that we are so afraid of losing God that we would rather pin him down to a definite place where we can be totally secure. This makes some basic assumptions about the very nature of God and about God's intentions. Is our God a God who hides or one who would be known by name? Is our God intent upon self-preservation or upon self-gift? And if we believe the former, is this a comment upon ourselves or upon God? I have suggested that believing people will ask questions and reflect upon the place of their experience in their search for God. Reflection is of the essence of any religious quest and its starting point will be what is accessible in order to go to what at first appears inaccessible. The God whom we learn gradually is the image in which we are made and our image is revealed to us in what we do as well as in what we are. The harmony of God's being and doing is such that it is expressed in gift rather than in acquisition, in giving rather than in taking.

If this is what God is like, then we may safely re-examine our assumptions. If this is what God is like, then we can safely look at our own lives and seek to believe in ways that do not fragment our experience, no longer dividing it into 'in church' and 'out of church', 'religious' and 'the rest'. This division represents a false dualism rather than an insight into the vision of God. It perpetuates the myth from which Jesus sought to free us. Some of the most fundamental of our assumptions relate to *where* we think God is. If we believe that God lives in church, then we will have to go to church to look for God. If we believe that God lives in nature, then we will have a hard job of it seeking and finding at the supermarket checkout point as we face another mindless and seemingly unending queue. If we believe that God lives in heaven, then the earth will be empty of God's presence. If we believe that God is everywhere and that the preferred dwelling place of God is within people, then we will look for God everywhere and above all in personal relationships.

The place and presence of God

The birth of Jesus should have dispelled our every doubt about where God is. The advent refrains of the Roman liturgy resonate to the words Mary heard from the angel, 'I, the holy one, am in the midst of you.' The Jesus who says, 'Come down Zacchaeus; today I will dwell at your house' (Luke 19.5), who tells John's two disciples to 'come and see' when they ask him 'Master, where do you dwell?' (John 1.39) is the word made flesh, come to dwell among us; the creative word who made our world in the first place, who found it good then and would continue to find it good now if only we did not shut him out so. It is not for nothing that Jesus' ministry began with a proclamation of this presence: 'Repent and believe, the Kingdom of God is in your midst' (Mark 1.15). Once God's involvement in human history has been accepted, the rest is somehow less complicated.

A God who is among us, everywhere rather than anywhere special, is a God who is interested in our experience, in our relationships, in our fears, our sorrows and our joys. For this reason the believing person will be a reflective person, a person who is committed to seeking and finding God in all things and people and situations. Usefully, therefore, we might ask how we can become more reflective, how we can become better seekers and better finders and thereby learn to pray.

What I mean by this is that, as women, we should not just reclaim our experience and celebrate it but that we should reflect upon it. This is important for two reasons: firstly, to be attentive to God's presence; and secondly, in order to make informed decisions rather than to act on impulse. What is implied is that our memory and imagination and dreams and feelings give us access to the place of harmony between our deepest desires and our transitory longings. In this place we find the presence of God within us and the freedom to live out of this understanding. In this place there can be no more stereotyping of any sort because all doing and being is received from a God whose justice begins to inform our every action. We can hear the call of God and the outlines of our own answers. From being people who pray by 'saying prayers', we become praying and discerning people.

What may seem surprising, however, is to be presented with this idea as an illustration of what happens when we begin to take the incarnation and the development of our own personal faith seriously and to see the connection between the two. What may seem surprising is the notion that sexual stereotyping has to be confronted at the level of faith rather than at the level of action. Action alone is not enough; what believing people say and do about women is a sign of the extent to which the reign of God is already coming to fulfilment in their hearts. Such belief is of the essence of conversion or growth towards God. The openness to God that comes about when we live as reflective people is a useful way to change gear, to move beyond categories that imprison ourselves and other people in roles, and which curtail the place and purpose of God in our world.

An extract from a favourite novel, *The Color Purple* by Alice Walker, says it so well that I think I will leave this Black American writer with the last word:

> Celie, tell the truth, have you ever found God in church? I never did. I just found a bunch of folks hoping for him to show. Any God I ever felt in church I brought in with me. And I think all the other folks did too. They come to church to *share* God, not find God.
>
> *The Color Purple* (The Women's Press 1983) p. 165

Attentive people who are committed to reflecting upon their experience, people who take God to church and are free to share God there as elsewhere, are people who are empowered to move beyond sexual stereotyping without any fear. They find personal value in who they are – people who seek and find God everywhere – rather than in the roles into which a sexist world or a sexist Church would push them. The faith of Christbearing women, women who enjoy the freedom to refer everything to God, is a gift to the Church. These are people who share a God who is known by name and, as such, prophets in our world. They do not idolize the hierarchies with which we have institutionalized the quest for power. They do not separate human experience, magicalizing some of it by calling it profane and sacramentalizing the rest by calling it religious. God's voice can be heard in the claim that the Lord has done such great things for these women. For Christ-bearing women praise and magnify a God whose love empowers us in all we are, in all we do and in all whom we love, a God who is the giver in every gift.

And this surely is the point. Not only is man not the normative human being, but likewise a male God is not the normative God. Where we try to encapsulate God by telling each other what God does in verbs that stereotype God's behaviour, too, then we relegate God to places in our lives where we are not in fact living, places that are peripheral, on the edges of our day-to-day experience. The images we have of prayer will in turn be programmed and limited by this understanding. For this reason chapter six will look at some of these and at how we may grow as praying women, as praying people. For the moment all that is implied is that the God who is and the God who does in our world needs the witness of both women and men. Where we are certain both of our identity and of the validity of our experience as a place where God is already at work and where God's call can already be heard, then can the reign of God begin.

3
Why do Women Serve?

∽

And the angels came and ministered to him
MARK 1.13

The serving Church

I have just prepared a reference for someone who is applying to be
selected for ordination to the diaconate in the Anglican Church. I
found myself having to do something which would have been
inconceivable even five years ago. That is to say I found myself
having to make a very clear distinction between the unordained
ministry she has already been doing as a lay university chaplain
and the ordained ministry to which she aspires. At the moment we
are witnessing an explosion of interest in Christian ministry, to the
extent even that it becomes possible to consider the former in one
chapter and the latter in another. There was a time when the only
ministry these Churches recognized and named as Christian was
the work of ordained priests and other male ministers or elders.
Much of the agitation on the part of those who seek to change the
Churches' ruling on the question of the ordination of women has
worked out of this same understanding. I believe that some of it is
ill-directed because it connives with the over-clerical reading of
Christian ministry which comes about when the work of priests is
the only form of Christian service recognized and made absolute in
the Churches. Much of the activity of other pressure groups which
seek to campaign against the ordination of women is equally
misdirected, and seemingly even less free from the attempt to
manipulate by using emotive language or words which tap hidden
fears.

There are other ways of looking at the question, ways that declericalize or laicize the whole idea of ministry and make it
available to all believers, whether ordained or not. There are ways

31

of looking at what we all do as people who are committed to adult faith that will help us to live out this faith in service of each other, as part of our personal response to the call of Christ. There are ways to integrate our everyday experience and daily living which can usefully be explored once we have learnt to recognize that there are many forms of service in the Church.

The wider question is, What constitutes ministry? And behind this there lurks a theological question: 'What is the Church?' Or even, 'Where is the Church?' Ten or even five years ago this was not difficult to answer. The Church had nice clean edges and was easy to identify. We saw the Roman Catholic Church on television when the Vatican Council was in session or when cardinals met in Rome to elect two popes in quick succession. The present pope in turn became a powerful visual image in the world media. We saw the Church of England at royal weddings or the Queen's silver jubilee, or when bishops were consecrated and their photograph appeared on the back of a newspaper. The Church was easy to see. Priests looked like priests, nuns like nuns; their work could be described in language familiar to us all: saying Mass, giving sermons, visiting the sick, teaching the children, and so on. We knew what we expected to hear the Church saying: things about sin and salvation, about loving your neighbour and trying to forgive your enemy, about heaven and eternity. We knew where the Church began and ended, and this usually had something to do with the building itself or with the official church personnel who worked out of this building or the local convent. We knew where religion began and ended, what belonged and what did not belong to the spiritual world whose existence we acknowledged whenever we said our prayers or treated Sunday as a special day.

More recently, these familiar images seem to have been shot down in flames, and by people from the inside at that. So we see concern expressed for the poor and marginalized, notably in Latin American countries, and the emergence of liberation theology. We see priests and nuns arrested at the boundary wires of nuclear bases, or closing down big presbyteries and convents. Documents appear with titles like 'Faith in the City' and subtitles that make assumptions we had forgotten were part of our heritage, such as, 'A Call for Action by Church and Nation'. Religion appears to have something to do with politics, politics with religion.

Equally, concern with Christian unity has begun to make the

distinctions between 'them' and 'us' feel fuzzy; not merely as a minority but more importantly as fellow believers, Roman Catholics from the heart of the ghetto I come from find that we have more in common with other Christians than we imagined. I remember attending a performance of the *Messiah* in Wells cathedral when I was twelve. During the interval the dean came out to lead us in the Lord's Prayer. I fell to my knees only to be reproached by my brother. 'We don't pray with these people,' he informed me. Both of us have moved a long way since then. There are other signs of change, too. I notice, for instance, that with the emergence of catechetical programmes that ask members of the parish to help prepare children for the Eucharist or for Confirmation, religious instruction has been dramatically laicized and is no longer something we expect the priest or the sisters to do behind closed doors. This involvement has spun off in all sorts of other directions as well: the Church as people of God means me and other ordinary people too; the Church as pilgrim people means that I can talk about my faith journey to God without sounding pretentious; the Church as servant means that I can take a new look at what I do in my everyday life and see it with new eyes. Religion is no longer localized, attached to a special place or group of people or even a special day. It has taken off, shaken and invaded the whole of life. God is there in our midst, at play in our world, creating and redeeming us, making us good and finding us good in ways we had forgotten or never learnt.

An entirely new relationship with the 'world' of everyday living is envisaged once this division into sacred and secular is dropped. The world is the place where I am called to make sense of everything the gospel says about being leaven or seed, a nurturing, growing presence in its midst. This world is not set over and against the Church; the Church and the world are in relationship not in opposition. The world is the place where I am called to live and move and have my Christian being. It is where I may become a Christbearing woman.

A sense of newness and of personal call from God have led many believers to see that we are now responsible for being the Church in the world as never before. The Church is not something that priests run but something that *I am* as an adult believer, something that *we are* as faith community. My life is lived in the ordinary world; God appears to care about the ordinary world. Suddenly the Church's descent from the shining heights of Mount Tabor to the dusty road to Emmaus makes sense. That is to say that there is a good Gospel precedent for what is happening at the moment; there are reasons why we may engage with the real world of people and events as the place where we become disciples of the risen Christ, and the incarnation itself has to be the first of them. Our model is a God who cares about the human condition to the extent of intervening in the human story; our model is a Jesus who is born, lives and dies as his way of growing to the fulness of life we call the resurrection; our model is a Holy Spirit who from the beginning has been hovering over the waters, getting broody over creation. This committed God calls for a committed Church, one in which Christian ministry is the norm rather than the exception. All of us, as people who share the universal call to holiness we received in baptism, can make a holy response to God, one which engages us at a far deeper level than the task-oriented response of flower-arranging or cleaning the church floor. People will continue to arrange flowers in church, people will continue to launder the altar linen, people will continue to read in church or celebrate the liturgy, but we will also arrange flowers in our own homes, wash clothes and cook meals to be eaten around other tables as our way of coming to God and building up the faith community. Being Church and making Church in all we are and do become the Christian task of all believers.

In so far as the Church in which most of us were raised was one that saw ministry as the responsibility of priests and was reluctant to share their control of divine resources with an untrained and theologically illiterate laity, certain other ideas necessarily followed. The desire behind this attitude may have been a sincere, even a holy one; that is to say religion was taken so seriously that any risk of 'debasing' it was regarded as sinful and wrong. It followed, therefore, that the only kind of faith response which lay people could enjoy was a devotional one. We were allowed to be preoccupied with the progress of our own souls, under the Church's guidance and with the help of the Church's sacraments. Indeed we were actively encouraged to worry about the state of our souls. My own earliest Christian memories are of singing the hymn 'Soul of my Saviour' with passionate conviction while my family went up to the altar rails to receive Communion. As I made my First Communion at the age of seven, this memory antedates that time. What I am saying is that even the youngest of children received from the Church the idea that *my* salvation and sanctification, *my* relationship with Jesus were all-important, and that any pious or deeply-felt reaction to the gift of divine life was to be experienced in terms of souls and certainly not in terms of bodies. I would gaze up into the remote roof of the church and worry about my soul. Was it as black as the ceiling I could dimly see up there and as big a barrier between me and God? By the age of eight I was singing 'I loved the garish day and, spite of fears, Pride ruled my will; remember not past years' from Newman's 'Lead Kindly Light' as though my life depended on it.

To sidetrack people into preoccupation with their own salvation is to mutilate the gospel message. Where Jesus spoke of loving God and loving one's neighbour in one and the same breath, he was suggesting that Christianity is about other people, and that self-love or self-acceptance is a prerequisite for any sincere loving or accepting of other people. Nowadays we use the word 'people' where the hymns of my childhood used the word 'soul'; nowadays we are concerned with seeking and finding God in relationships with other people, and consequently we can take much more seriously what Jesus had to say about looking after each other in his name. Certain of the ways in which we look after each other are so evidently rituals: those to do with keeping people clean and clothed and fed, with accompanying them through the rites of passage as they grow into adult life and so to the rite of death. It follows that ministry is not an additional extra – a special service from an élite corps – rather ministry is a word the Church has been given to describe all Christian care and service. Such service is of the essence of Christian presence in the world; it is the way in which we make Church.

Reclaiming ministry

And so ministry is to be reclaimed by all those who offer such care and service as part of their everyday way of coming to God and of bringing others to God. Like the angels in Mark's account of the temptations, we minister to Jesus in all we do as Christians. Every action can be reclaimed once the way we seek to find God stops being both over-spiritualized and over-privatized. By this I mean that faith is not about me and God, even less is it about my soul and God. Rather it is about how I seek and find God in the world constituted by my family and friends and the people on my street or on my TV screen; it is about how I live and move and have my being as a Christian woman to whom God has given a real, live context, certain real, live relationships, a real body and a real world. To see faith otherwise is to reduce the activity of God to some realm called the 'spiritual', to deny that we are whole people with arms and legs and hands and feet, let alone with loving hearts. To see faith otherwise is to refuse to love my neighbour and merely to persist in the pagan attitude of keeping other people out of my life as far as possible or, if I do let them in, of screening and selecting them for my personal enjoyment. Only God qualifies for admittance, not the people with whom I am asked to share a sign of peace in God's name, and certainly not the person who is set on by thieves and who lies in the gutter at my feet, nor the one whose wounds are licked by the dogs at my front door.

If this is what faith is all about, then those who have a great deal to do with other people are well-placed to begin to see their lives in terms of ministry or service. 'Blessed are the homemakers, for the reign of God is in your midst . . .' 'Blessed are the attentive, those who find time to listen and to sympathize, those who invest themselves in the well-being of others . . .' How are people to know that God loves them if we do not love them ourselves? The gospel transforms both the reason why, and the way in which, we perceive other people. The gospel speaks of forms of service which honour both those who serve and those to whom such service is given.

Christian presence as gospel presence

The word ministry, in effect, is more than a useful standard around which to invite people to rally. Both a theology and some guidelines for the practice of personal relationships have to be examined where we are committed to these as believing adult people. The theology is about making God present and finding God present, about being committed to the incarnation as it finds expression in our own Church and world. In every person we meet or have dealings with, we are, with the angels, ministering to Jesus. That is to say that friendship and love and companionship are part of the very fabric of the Christian life. When such people are in pain or asking questions, then our presence in their midst is an additional guarantee of God's presence to them. When we are confused or angry or full of doubt and they listen to us, then the same obtains. This answers the question 'Why?' What then about the question 'How?' How are we to make faith community or be Church in this way? Part of an answer can be clarified by looking again at the angels who come to minister to Jesus.

I have suggested that in our lived experience or personal and collective memory, ministry was understood uniquely as the task of clerics, with its terms of reference defined by ordained men. We spoke about church services as though they were the only genuine ones, and sacramentalized the rites of passage. Those who ministered, dressed as angels; that is to say they put on long white dresses in order to officiate: white as a symbol of purity, dresses to cover them up. But angels are more than bodiless beings. They are places where God is made present and can visit the world; they are little incarnations. Michael's strength, Raphael's healing and Gabriel's word bring God to the Jewish people's terror in the face of their Persian enemy, to Tobias' need as he struggles with penury in exile from his own country, and to the home of the young Jewish woman, Mary. Biblical angels do not live in church, they are out and about strengthening, healing and speaking to people. Whatever they do is directed to helping people experience the action of God in their lives and to bringing God's message to these people where they are and as they are. If these angels' capacity to relate to the world is non-sexual, this is because they are committed to a variety of relationships, each one appropriate to the individual they meet in God's name. Above all they are not afraid of getting their hands dirty; angels would not understand our use of the word angelic. The angels who minister to Jesus are out there in the wilderness where he is; they are prepared to go out beyond the safety of the city to the place of temptation.

This has something important to say, I believe, to Christian people whose way of coming to God and bringing others to God is to be out and about in the world strengthening, healing and speaking to others. This work is familiar to all those who minister at the level of family and friends, of home and neighbourhood rather than at the level of structure and institution. Those who work in institutions know that, essentially, they are about people. But nevertheless it remains true to say that structures all too readily get in the way of people; even families can get in the way of the growth of their individual members. Where, however, we begin to see everything we do as Christians as a way of bringing about the incarnation again and again in today's world, then the ministry of lay women, the ministry of lay men, the ministry of the ordained and that of religious can all be reclaimed by the Churches and our structures transformed.

Jesus himself demythologizes ministry in that he resolutely keeps it at the level of people and their needs. Christian presence turns out to be about spending time being with people so that in the fulness of time we may feed, heal and teach those who are hungry, sick and ignorant – whether of learning or of love. His presence is guaranteed in the world by the Spirit breathed into the Body of his new creation, and found now wherever believers are present in his name. His Body is committed to feed, heal and teach and thereby continue the choice he made in becoming a human person in the first place. Moreover where, necessarily, he was committed to choosing a male body the first time round, now he is found in women and men, in children and in old people, in the sick, the handicapped, the imprisoned, in those who minister and in those to whom they minister in his name.

Wherever there are people in need and the presence of Christ is made available to them in the presence of believers, then the Church ministers. This ministry is not about church people looking after other church people, about servicing a bureaucracy. It is about becoming Christbearers in the world, about taking one's membership of the human family seriously. For this reason, some of those who minister will be people who see justice issues in terms that do not match our own. Some of those who minister will necessarily go to groups of people whom the world despises. The call of Christ is an insistent one and this is how they hear it. Some of those who minister will never go beyond their own front doors; all those who come to them, however, are made welcome in the name of Christ. I have heard this openness parodied, heard people say that ministry is trivialized where every gesture Christians make is to be understood as the work of a Christ who still labours in our world. Yet the Jesus who speaks from Matthew's Gospel is prepared to name the giving of a cup of water as ministry, and I would be reluctant to want either to clericalize or to dismiss that.

A while ago the Roman Catholic newspapers carried a piece under the heading 'Video Nice' about a film being prepared by a diocesan seminary on the formation of young men who are preparing for the priesthood. This film would open, we were told, with wholesome shots of young men coming in from an afternoon of football to eat a hearty tea and then talk earnestly about their devotional life and the inspiration they were finding in their years of formal study for ministry. I felt uncomfortable as I read the report and only discovered why when I began to consider what opening shots I instinctively thought might be more appropriate for such a film. The lead came a couple of months later when I was standing on the platform of a suburban underground station waiting for the train to grind in. Opposite me on an equally deserted platform a young black boy shifted an empty Coca-Cola can from one foot to the other, fidgeting restlessly for a full ten minutes before I recognized what was staring me in the face. Anyone who looked bored, cold and lonely is making a statement about the human condition, about our need for meaning and companionship. What better place to begin a film about working at the level of human need than with a shot which makes this point?

A similar perspective is that envisaged by Ignatius Loyola in his *Spiritual Exercises*, in a text he called the 'Contemplation on the Incarnation':

> I will try to enter into the vision of God, in his triune life, looking upon our world: men and women aimless, despairing, hateful and killing, men and women sick and dying, the old and the young, the rich and the poor, the happy and the sad, some being born and some being laid to rest. The leap of divine joy: God knows that the time has come when the mystery of his salvific plan, hidden from the beginning of the world, will become manifest.
>
> David L. Fleming SJ, tr., *The Spiritual Exercises*
> (Institute of Jesuit Sources, St Louis, 1978), p. 71

God looks at our world lovingly and sees real people with real needs to visit and fulfill. The despair of those who search for meaning and cannot find it is a cry for help which this God can understand. The intervening God whom Ignatius of Loyola saw gazing upon the world from heaven is moved to action by the human condition and this God's first answer is to not to come covered with muscle and might but just to be born, to choose to be present in the world in the most simple way possible, as a baby. The message must be that our first reaction to people is to seek to be present with them to whatever it is that frightens them or fills them with joy. Christian ministry is first of all about presence and only secondly about doing things. All too often we supply the latter without being attentive to the former; we seem to prefer sound to silence, activity to awareness. The people who have ministered most effectively to me when I have been in need have often adopted such a low-key approach that to the casual observer they might have seemed positively inattentive. In fact, however, they were there noticing and supporting and, when necessary, asking the simple question, 'Are you all right?' at just the right time.

My experience has been that people who value and seek to grow in relationships are well placed to minister, whether they are women or men. In this context above any other we are committed to growing in human ways, within time, as the people we are. This is the context in which cups of water or tea come into their own. Culturally women enjoy something of an advantage in that we have been allowed to 'bond' and explore the experience of human inter-relatedness, partly because another more competitive model of interaction has been chosen by men. Clearly this is not true of all women nor of all men. Nevertheless there are ways in which women have been freed to develop, there are models of care and service we have been able to create which are part of a tradition the Churches have yet to integrate into the mainstream of their life. This tradition stands in the same relationship to the formal organized tradition of priestly ministry as personal faith does to organized religion. It has the same values and concerns.

The most important of these is a concern to be with other people as they go through the rites of passage, that is to say as they grow up and learn the joys and responsibilities of answering the call to become fully human and fully alive. To be with people who are in pain or who are in love or who are anxious and troubled, questioning, grieving or at peace means helping them to identify their feelings by being available to listen to them as they talk. To provide opportunities in this way is to minister at the level of the individual rather than the group and thereby to accompany rather than to lead. This means that people are helped both to have and to reflect upon their own experience, to discover the meaning to it which may or may not later be celebrated in sacramental practice or anything that happens in church.

The model of human development behind this understanding is

one where movement will be from dependence through independence to interdependence. The fully autonomous person can be rather an odious individual. I do not recognize in him the Jesus who began his public ministry by choosing friends to work with, friends to call his own. I do not recognize in him the Jesus who loved women and died in their company. Personal one-to-one ministry to human growth cannot have this autonomy as its goal. Women bear children from their most vulnerable beginning through to the first experience of dependence. In Western Europe and the cultures formed from Western Europe we have also had a prime role in helping children develop and grow through this initial dependency; we have been midwives to their development into independence. Beyond that, however, we have continued to desire companionship and friendship and love, and in this we have had our way. I believe that this tradition is a resource the Churches have yet to understand and feed upon.

Development through any rites, whether of passage or of what feels more like a dead end, takes place in time. Our ordinary way of marking time is to use the patterns given us by the sun: to value the light more than the dark and to notice the seasons because they recall the return of light, the place of light in our lives. Where we rely so heavily upon the twenty-four hour clock and expect to feel better again in the same day our expectations are tailored only to one clock. We are the victims of *chronos*. Inside each of us, however, there lurks that other clock, and perhaps we have to be at the bottom of a pit to know that it exists. It is a clock that can only be seen in the dark, when a moon is visible which waxes and wanes in twenty-eight-day cycles. This clock, as I have intimated, is more generous with time and measures it off in quite different quantities. It says that each day does not have to have the same feel and shape, the same pace and mood. It allows for flexibility, for rhythms of creativity and rest. It is a rhythm of give and take, of ebb and flow. Above all it is a rhythm which reminds us that the place of life is within, that we are reborn and revivified from within, from the place of living waters we all carry in our inner space. People who come to us when they are feeling down and depressed, or when they are feeling cheerful, are asking for access to that inner space within themselves, and the lessons of the dark are as valid as the lessons of the light. My own experience is that women have a special role in helping people to discover the existence of this inner clock because they have a lived experience of its workings.

Whole ministry

For understandings such as these to find expression in the Churches' life and practice is very freeing. God's work is done in God's way when it is shared by both women and men, because the God in whose image and likeness we are made finds fuller expression in whole ministry than in partial and clerical ministry. Beyond the hierarchies of sexism or clericalism both women and men, the lay and the ordained, can help each other live more fully as Christian presence in God's world. In this way the incarnation has a more truly human face and the Kingdom comes more convincingly. Any other understanding limits the action of God and puts up barriers within our experience of this action. Any other understanding makes an incomplete statement about God and God's desire to intervene, to be present to human reality.

And this surely is the point. The God we image will be experienced as an interested God or as an alien God only to the extent to which named Christians are prepared to give face and form to everything Jesus said in the Gospels about loving each other in his name. For this reason, too, it is helpful when we take more seriously the quality of our being in the world because then the way we serve the world will be informed by this quality of presence. If ministry is about strengthening, healing and speaking to others, then those who have learnt to take their identity and experience seriously have the further insight that, in the relationship between the two, they have not found themselves to be strong, healthy, articulate people, but people who can distinguish the true from the false. Real strength, real health and real fluency with words come from the person who has learnt self-acceptance, not the person who is struggling to earn God's favour. The burden of false models of Christian presence is one we can all afford to lose, and this insight can transform everything the Churches are and do in ordinary homes and ordinary workplaces, let alone what actually happens in church buildings each Sunday. People who make Church like this can help the body of believers to experience itself as serving and servant. In this way the question of what constitutes the Christian vocation can receive a realistic answer, as chapter seven will try to suggest.

4
Why do Women Celebrate?

⤳

And some he called apostles and some disciples
LUKE 6.13

Naming and knowing

The Jesus who names, like Adam in the Genesis story, is a Jesus who identifies the gifts of God. In turn, where we name we enter into relationships with what or whom we name and make a statement about our deepest beliefs and attitudes. People whom we know by name have become part of our own personal reality, part of the fabric of our lives; situations we know by name, even frightening ones, are somehow less chaotic when we are able to identify them and find how they belong. We know from experience that the deepest of emotions and feelings give us a range of words we use with care, because the reality they describe is so precious. So we do not throw words like 'love' and 'death', 'delight' and 'grief' around lightly. We entrust them only to those who know how to use them to speak the truth, because the truth alone can set us free.

Yet even the most ordinary and everyday of words has also to be used carefully, otherwise we introduce elements of disorder into our lives that serve only to complicate them. We need to name even our simplest needs with care; to ask for bread when we mean bread and a stone when we mean a stone. We need to answer our needs with equal care. 'Who among you, if your child asked for bread would give him a stone?' (Matt. 7.9). The malice implied in this kind of misunderstanding is contrasted by Jesus with his experience of the Father's way of understanding him and answering his needs. Right now I find myself asking, what we are asking of God when we begin to talk about ordination? What kind of image or understanding are we describing?

43

My least favourite image is of ordination as a rugby ball. In Rome, and in certain branches of the Anglican communion, 'orders' are a thing that people, well, men, pass to each other – and usually backwards – in a public place. I imagine that a number of people will recognize in is image something of their own experience of the way the Church seems to treat the gift God gave us to name some as priests. It goes against what the tradition also tells us; that all the baptized share the priesthood in which Jesus alone is truly priest. There is only one priest and the work of our redemption has been done by this priest. The priesthood we share as baptized people allows us to teach each other and feed each other and care for each other in his name. It also enables us to name this gift in certain individuals, to train them and support them in the specific work they do in our service.

I suppose really that this is why the rugby ball image just will not do. Priesthood is not a thing, a possession that some people have and that others do not. Jesus alone knows and names things and people completely truly before God; he alone is in true relationship with his Father and with the whole of reality, so he alone can bring each element of creation into harmony and identify true needs before God. Jesus as priest intercedes for us all, women as well as men. In Jesus God's love is shaped to human need. Above all, he helps heal our images and partial understanding of God's gifts.

I used to feel very strongly about the question of the ordination of women. By strongly I suppose I mean I felt militant about the fact that women should be ordained. But now I am less happy with some of my indignation because it was misdirected. My attention was focused upon the question of orders as a thing: why should this thing be refused to women? Why should we not be allowed to exercise the ministry of ordained priests? Now I recognize that I, too, was looking at ordination as an object or possession, as something some people have and others do not, and I was trying to guarantee that this thing should be made available to women – though not, I should add, to me personally.

Then I had a vocation to that kind of priesthood, was dazzled for a while and then, lo and behold, began to see what was going on and where it was leading me. The vocation came during a very solemn liturgy, the Easter Vigil celebrated in a perfect setting. I gazed into a sanctuary full of men, stiff with the brilliance of their brocaded vestments, and wanted to be up there too. My only misgiving came at the moment when the Easter candle was plunged into the bowl of waiting water. The Roman Catholic Easter Vigil service is full of wonderful elemental imagery about fire and water, dark and light, and some of its sexual overtones or pre-Christian origins are fairly explicit. If anyone was going to be raped in public did I really want to join the violaters? The vocation began to fade.

Within a year I had discovered a different way of looking at things, one where the ministry of all the baptized was to be redeemed and valued as an expression of the universal call to holiness which has been emphasized, for instance, by the Roman Catholic Church since the Second Vatican Council. This distracted me from the question of the ordination of women for at least the next two years, and then something began to change. I began to notice that the refusal of the two Churches I know best – my own and the Anglican Church in England – was saying something very important to me about how they saw women, and so the focus of my concern moved away from ordination as object or thing and moved on towards women as people before God.

I began to see certain connections and to envisage certain comparisons. For instance, in the sacrament of reconciliation God's forgiveness of a given individual is named by the Church in the person of the priest. This forgiveness is available before the individual asks for it, yet the sacrament gives the certainty that this is so. The sacrament is not a piece of magic, the priest does not wave a wand over the rather messy business of my life-to-date when I go to confession. It is not an object either, not a thing which at one moment I do not have and then at the next I do. Rather it is making a complete statement about God and about me as an individual whom God loves and reconciles at all times, about my world and all the people in it whom God is reconciling at all times. The sacrament names me as at once sinner and as forgiven. It says that we are in relationship, that I can know God.

What happens when that same way of looking at things is applied to the sacrament of ordination? I have described my own conversion on the question in a certain amount of detail because I believe it may speak to the experience of a number of people; married men and women, for instance, as well as to single women. My point is that when we view sacraments as things, we really do make them into objects, special packets of God's grace which some people have and others do not. Only a headlong fall into that mentality, and then the misgivings that come with the sense of where this is leading one – in my case, into real connivance with an attitude to which in my heart of hearts I did not subscribe and which appalled me when I reflected on it – only this kind of error gives the impetus to come to conversion. The pattern goes something like this, I believe: time is needed for any conversion to take root, and God is good. In continuing to inform what is happening in other ways, God gradually lets the really important questions surface again and clamour for attention.

Women and sacramental practice

These important questions about sacraments and priesthood have to do with naming women before God. Where the Churches refuse ordination to women, where they say of women that they are unordainable, what are they saying about God and what are they saying about women? If sacraments are ways in which God names people and shares this naming with the Church, if they are this rather than magic, then the root question becomes, can women know God and bring God into the lives of others, bring others before God? Is there a real relationship possible between them? For naming is tied to knowing, the one pre-supposes the other. And what we are doing when we celebrate sacraments is surely naming God and our experience of God's intervention in our lives.

Part of the thinking behind this way of looking at sacraments is obscured because we base so much of our sacramental thinking upon the way in which, at present, we celebrate or experience the Eucharist. Yet no one turns a hair when a nurse or a midwife or mother exercises her priestly function by baptizing a new-born child. No one turns a hair when the sacrament of matrimony is given by one apparently unordained person to another. The new-born child is baptized in a hurry or in private, so perhaps the truth of the matter is that we do not ordinarily reflect on what this is saying about priesthood. The couple who marry each other do so in the presence of someone ordained so that what is happening is somehow concealed. So much ceremony surrounds the wedding itself that we do not ordinarily reflect on the fact that marriages are consummated only in time. They have patterns and rhythms which extend both forward and backwards from the moment of consent celebrated in church. Nevertheless it remains true that in either instance, what is being done is a certain kind of naming – of individuals and relationships before God. In baptism and matrimony, where such naming is of a most elemental sort – that is to say that it describes primary relationships towards God and towards each other – we seem to have no difficulty about letting women do the naming. We acknowledge that they do indeed know God and that their presence is indispensible where God's gift in birth or marriage is celebrated.

Insights such as this enable us to think in new ways about what is going on when we talk about ordination. They are part of the creativity which comes in the wake of listening to new voices in the Church. Such creativity would seem to be an essential if men, too, are to be liberated from false images and understandings that constrain them to see themselves as possessers of God and God's ways. Where we acknowledge that women can know God, we are also saying that God can know women and can know the experience of women. This is not a plea for a return to seeking and finding God among the saucepans, but for a new way of looking at what we do when we celebrate our need of God.

What begins to happen when we ask women to name God, to say 'This is the word of the Lord' and 'This is my body' where they are already able to say 'I baptize you' or 'I take you to be my husband'? What begins to happen when our ability to name is extended to the eucharistic table as well? The first time I attended a Eucharist celebrated by a woman I have to admit that I was distracted by the little pink suede shoes the pastor was wearing. I resented this and wanted to feel very pious and to have the reactions I have ordinarily when a man is celebrating. Instead I was forced to concede that someone like me and someone who shares my enjoyment of the colour pink was celebrating that fact along with everything else she was celebrating. All my ideas were being tested. In theory I am prepared to say that I believe that life is the primary sacrament, that there is no division into sacred and secular, but here I was resisting the experience when it really began to happen for me. I found myself wanting to sacramentalize what was going on, to make it remote rather than actual. In this way I was necessarily magicalizing the little pink suede shoes, as though they did not belong.

Celebrating sacraments

For years I had begun lessons on the sacraments by asking my pupils to list the most important moments in any human being's life. Birth and death were obvious front runners. The more reflective children would look at their own experience and note down things like their first day at infant school or at secondary school. The more precocious would grope around for a suitable euphemism and come up with something like 'my first kiss', start giggling and then opt more frankly for the word 'sex'. Birth, death, the ability to form relationships and eventually to give sexual expression to those relationships clearly seemed to them to be the most important of human experiences. Then came something about the whole process of growing up, the experience of pain and depression, of change and the quest for identity.

Only when these had been listed did we move on to look at the way God visits those needs through the sacraments the Church celebrates at present, because only then were my pupils able to see that the sacraments accompany human growth and indicate God's concern and interest in the process whereby we become fully alive. The most everyday sacrament of all, the thanksgiving or Eucharist, is the one that is saying this most clearly. In this sense it is the one that most clearly asks for a whole priesthood.

To appeal for 'whole priesthood' like this is to domesticize the very notion of priesthood, and at the same time to remove barriers between religion in church and religion in the home. This suggests that present-day interest in basic or local Christian communities is necessarily going to throw up different models of priesthood anyway and that the experience women have of knowing God-in-the-round as it were, of seeking and finding and celebrating God in real situations, at real tables and in real relationships, has prepared them to be priest in a totally new way. The person for others who names things in and for the community of faith of the local church is likely to do so accurately if she or he knows both the wider context of all belief (that is to say, the tradition of the universal Church), and as well the men, women and children, the old people, the sad people, the rejoicing people of the neighbourhood.

Much of our present-day experience of what a priest should or should not do, of what he is or is not like, owe more to paganism than to the model given by Jesus, the only priest. The pagan priest intercedes with an angry God; the pagan priest calls down fire or carves up victims. Physical strength of a certain kind appears to be mandatory if he is to humour God and offer appropriate sacrifices. And this is the point: the pagan priest serves a pagan God. If we continue to set up priests like this, by saying they have to be men and that their job is inappropriate for women, then we are betraying the essentially pagan image we have of God. The sacrificing priesthood serves a hostile God and the work of our redemption remains undone.

What if God were not like that? What if God were concerned to set up a tent in our midst and dwell among us? God the home-maker lays a different kind of table, one around which people come to talk and laugh and share, to taste and to see that the Lord is good. God the homemaker puts the kettle on and draws up chairs. God the homemaker wants to hear about the real problems and questions that exercise us, about the people we love and the people we fear. How is the presence of this God to be mediated in our midst? The answer cannot be in terms of the traditional image of priest which we have portrayed as the only one. Different images of God generate different styles of ordained ministry. Ordained to what? Ordained to the service of whom? These are legitimate questions.

The word 'mediated' bothers me slightly because it sets priests apart as people who stand between me and God. Perhaps this is because some of my experience has been of 'priest as obstacle' rather than of 'priest as vehicle' of God's presence in my life. I resent the fact that the Church has canonized the foundress of a religious Order whose sisters serve as priests' housekeepers, while resolutely refusing to canonize other foundresses whose insights into the nature of Christian presence in the world challenge that way of looking at things, not to mention that particular vision of Christian service and of complementarity. I prefer the interpreta-tion of the Martha and Mary story which understands the better part that Mary has chosen as the challenging one of taking her rightful place at the feet of the rabbi. She flouts the convention which says that this place is reserved for men and sits to learn at Jesus' feet. Not because she is into sitting at men's feet, but because she has seen that she can use the rabbinic way of learning within the context of her own home. She vindicates both the idea that women may know and learn God – the prerogative apparently of priests – and the idea that they may do so at home.

The domestic setting turns out to be an apt one. From this one story the enthusiast might be tempted to list all the homes into which Jesus went, all the domestic settings in which he chose to make the reign of God present – from the home of Peter's mother-in-law, to that of Jairus – but in a sense this is not the point. The point has something to do with the difference this makes to our own practice.

Priests as vehicles, and this means both men and women priests, can name God as surely in the church as in the home, in the street as in the supermarket. Their focus is less on the place than on the people they are meeting there. In their naming they are both identifying experience as the place where they meet God and entering into relationship with the people who have this experience. The very first celebration of this style of Christian presence recorded for us is that of the two disciples on the way to Emmaus. One of these disciples is named for us; he is called Cleopas. The other is not, so I will call her the wife of Cleopas because her name has been withheld from me. Here are people who are in relationship, who are able to share their hopes and fears, their joys and mistakes. As they walk long, naming their condition before God, Jesus begins to walk with them and so is able to come into their home and sit down at their table. Only there, however, can they name him when they recognize him in the breaking of the bread. The experience they lived in Jerusalem and out on the street finds some sort of focus when it is brought together around the Christian table. Jerusalem represents the religion of sacrifice, to which Jesus too was sacrificed; Emmaus represents the religion of presence, just as Bethlehem had. Each throws up different models of priesthood because each throws up different models of whatever it is that is the centre of the Christian message. What is the most important thing that Jesus did for us? Be born for us, or die for us? If the latter, then obviously death and dying and sacrifice and immolation and self-denial move to the centre of our Christian understanding. If the former, then being born and living and being human and concerned with the people around us, building each other up and nurturing each other and learning to live well in order to die well, are likely to seem important to us. The Christbearer is always a pain-bearer but never a masochist.

Priests who minister to our human growth as believing people are committed to working at the level of person rather than the level of institution, at the level of home and street rather than the level of church premises. This is territory familiar to women, and so I find myself wondering how long it will be before the formal, hierarchical Church recognizes something which a lot of people already know intuitively; that God can be known and named in new ways by those whose tent happens to be pitched there. I suppose, though, that this is part of the problem. The de-institutionalization of religion which will take place when women are ordained *in numbers* can feel fairly threatening. Can we face the fact that God will move out of church, that what we celebrate at every meal, every time we say to each other that we are sorry, every time we make love, will somehow be opened right up as a profoundly religious experience? Can we reconcile what we know of God already with what we suddenly find we are learning from scratch? If human life is really what we celebrate when we meet around the Lord's table, can we face the consequences?

One of these consequences is that what we do when not in church and not around the Lord's table has somehow to be reflected upon and integrated into the way in which we come to God in any formal context. Priests whose task it is to minister to the faith response of those in their pastoral care have a responsibility here which calls out responses for which it is very difficult to train people in seminaries and theological colleges. Immersion and integration are words that spring more readily to mind than withdrawal and study as traditionally conceived. Many priests, as trained at present, have been isolated from human realities and their own human responses in the name of some higher good. Many have been formed for one Church and are expected to work in another. No wonder they feel both fragmented and threatened by all this talk of women priests.

The restoration of the priesthood to some sort of wholeness would, however, ensure that both women and men would receive appropriate training and appropriate scope once trained for tomorrow's priesthood. Until women are ordained in numbers, there will be no real shift of emphasis. Once they are ordained, the training and ministry and on-going training of priests will take on quite different forms, ones that reflect the level of engagement in the human story which is required of them by the nature of what they celebrate.

Intimations of what this might mean are already being seen where in-service training schemes for the ordained work well. Men who have gone through first formation and who are beginning to realize that it has left holes in the way they react to people and situations and things, are enabled to take their own personal and human growth more seriously. This is because they can meet and share as equals and discuss what it is that is really important in their lives. What is sad is that many people have had to wait well beyond regular seminary or theological college to give attention to their own personal needs. I would argue that if women were training alongside men in college, that if women were working alongside men as fellow priests, this need not happen. Confrontation and intimacy with people of a different sex is a great catalyst to human development. More importantly, the cultural experience of women is such that they are able to cut through much of the theological muscle-flexing that goes on when men clerics meet. They have learnt that what they know, quantitively, is less important than how they know it and what they are doing with their knowledge.

Personal development such as this takes account of the fact that we are changing all the time, that faith really does commit us to grow. Present-day understanding of ongoing revelation is not just a smart way of saying that the Church is committed to growth and to change. More importantly we have to accept that we, too, are all the time being revealed to ourselves, that we can grow in self-knowledge and in the love of God and each other, that we grow in self-knowledge and change as people as we come to a fuller understanding of vocation within the Church. In Churches where women are already being ordained these lessons are being internalized in ways that confront the fundamental questions: Can women know God? And, Who is this God whom they know by name?

Both for the priesthood itself and for the Church or people whom priests are ordained to serve the ordination of women is perhaps not the great bogey it is feared to be. 'Can women know God?' is as great a question as 'Can men know God?' The naming both men and women do of God and of each other goes a long way towards suggesting what any individual's personal answer is. In either case, the answer the Churches give will make a considerable difference to the way they perceive the sacraments and sacramental practice.

Certain sacraments demand a church setting and a public context. Where our intention is to celebrate the gift of new life and to name a baby as a member of a Christian family the local parish makes an appropriate setting. The naming of a new relationship between two people who love each other likewise demands a public setting. The naming of God's forgiveness seems to ask for a variety of settings – some private, some public – and the anointing of the sick an equal variety. Confirmation is more tricky because we seem to be so uncertain as to what this sacrament means. The Spirit has already been given before any young man or woman is confirmed, just as the Spirit had already been given to the world on the dying breath of Jesus before any celebration of Pentecost. If young people need anything they need the privacy of anonymity, the possibility of being part of a group or a crowd. Yet at the same time they also need individual ministry, personal attention from named people who undertake to be with them as they journey into adulthood. The system of sponsors or godparents admits of this, but we have not really developed its practice in particularly creative ways. We have not really looked at the 'one-step' theory which demonstrates that the best people to walk with me are those who are just one step ahead of me, rather than light years away from me and from where I am.

Sacramental practice has been extensively revised over the past twenty years; the way we talk about the sacraments has not yet really caught up with the way we celebrate them. Where, as one friend commented, we used to have the meaning and miss out on the experience, we are now in danger of having the experience and missing out on the meaning. What does God mean in giving us the ability to symbolize our encounters with the divine life we have within? What does God mean by making us as physical people with a real-life context, as people who can meet God in this context and in the relationships we enjoy there? How can we celebrate what we know? How can our priests help us celebrate what we know, help us value the experience and know its inner meaning and place in our lives? How can they help us know that God names and knows us and that we may name and know God?

Conclusion

So far my interest in the first part of this book has been on questions about who women are before God and who God is for us; about serving God and knowing God. I have said that my own attention has been directed to them because they are the principal questions raised by Christian feminism. However I also contend that each of them is bound to stay with us too if we fail to see that the real problem does not lie in the fact that God makes some of us women and some of us men. The real place of concern is the fear that lies within us, a fear that resents differences and sees them only in terms of power games. All questions about God are questions about the limits of our faith. Do we really believe that God loves us as we are, that God feels our anxiety and our pain and yet is ill at ease with our fear? Do we really believe that we are made in the image and likeness of a God in whom women can see themselves mirrored and find glory?

Instead of valuing the differences that God has given us, it seems to me that we create artificial differences to hide from the vision of God. We create vain fears to avoid living creatively out of love. Within them we take up extreme positions, choosing to make too clear a distinction between what is certainty and what is doubt, between what is sacred and what is secular, between having a vocation to some sort of formal ministry and not having such a vocation, between whatever is clerical and whatever is lay. A middle road does exist between each of these alternatives and this middle way is one that heals rather than exaggerates divisions. It enables both women and men to reclaim themselves as people God knows and loves and in whom God recognizes the divine image. It honours the vision of God.

Furthermore, I believe that it offers realistic possibilities for growth, and as such must be explored more carefully in the second part of the book. Important questions to do with who we are as people who say we believe, as people who want to pray, as people who want to know and name God in God's everyday coming into our world, and as people who want to form faith community or Church, have already been raised in this first part. The second part will attempt to sketch some answers.

Part Two

5

On being
a Believing Woman

Faith and practice

Most of us learnt to believe before we learnt to practise our belief in
any church setting. We learnt to say the word 'I' before we learnt
to say the word 'God'. The experience of the contexts in which we
learnt these words is worth reflecting on, because each of us has
them and they are very influential. Who first taught us about
ourselves and about God? From whom did we learn how to pray?
Most of us can remember women from our childhood who struck
us as being holy people, people who really were in relationship
with a God whom they knew and loved and talked to most of the
time. Often they did not know particularly much about God in the
sense of knowing facts about God, but their faith was a growing
one, in depth rather than certainty. The influence of these women
is an integral if sometimes unacknowledged part of our own faith
development. They modelled belief for us and also various kinds
of religious practice.

The experience of putting out little nuts in my grandmother's
garden for the birds and ringing the angelus to invite them to come
and eat; the experience of visiting her as she was dying and finding
that she was to be buried in her First Communion silk stockings,
carefully saved for this occasion from the event over eighty years
earlier; the experience of lighting candles at the back of the church
after Mass; the experience of morning and night prayers by my
bed; of being drowned in holy water when driving devout (or
maybe just plain nervous) passengers; each of these is part of the
mythology of my own upbringing and that of certain Roman
Catholic friends. Other examples reflect the experience of other
traditions, but are still instances of times when genuine piety
found expression in a variety of forms of religious practice, and

believing people from our childhood taught us to know God. What is significant, however, is that in the case of women in particular much of this religious practice formed part of a culture that was alternative to the formal culture of church religion. The practices I have referred to here were fringe activities, ways in which people like my grandmother sought to celebrate within the context of their own home, and invented their own liturgies. They form part of a tradition which could co-exist alongside the tradition represented by texts such as those quoted at the beginning of chapter one. The formal tradition of the hierarchical Church was supplemented by a tradition that enabled people to come to God in their own way and in their own time. Ordinarily it was developed by women, and in a certain sense it belonged to women.

This subculture was strong because it was by and large oral; people who had time to talk to each other had time to transmit it. A priest came to bless my grandmother's house when she moved into it. At the end of the visit we found that she had little corn dollies pinned behind each door, made according to a design from the Normandy of her childhood and learnt God alone knows how. When she died she was wearing two rows of medals on her nightdress; to the left, medals of St Thérèse of Lisieux, to the right those of Pius X. 'My saints', she informed me. Her contemporaries certainly – St Thérèse was only three years older than her and came from the same part of France – but what else was she trying to tell me? Something important, I believe, especially when she talked of cutting me out of her will when I entered the convent. Formal orthodoxy, which suddenly I was to represent, would name her own religious practice and call it pagan and superstitious.

With the Second Vatican Council, in particular, came movements that discarded nineteenth-century religious art and pious images; the formal tradition gained a kind of cultural supremacy. Silk stockings were no longer worn. In the Roman Catholic community the angelus and the rosary went out and in came the Eucharist and, at a pinch, the Divine Office. We were treated to sacramental sandwiches where people were married during Mass, baptized during Mass, confirmed and buried during Mass, even where each of these sacraments in fact could be celebrated in isolation. We took religion out of the home and drove it back into church when we suppressed forms of piety that could flourish in the domestic context. A new tyranny of practice replaced the old. This new practice centres on words about God as opposed, say, to gestures or silence for God and with God. Not only have we retreated into church but once there we have become one-dimensional, as our discovery of the word has led us to drop all the smells and sights and sounds and feelings with which, in this context at least, we had previously celebrated our humanness before God and had had a more diffused sense of God's activity in the congregation at prayer. In church at present the congregation is far more aware of the men who people the sanctuary because liturgical reform has focused our attention on the action there. Men are what one sees and hears; they have greater access to the word. Some kind of reaction is inevitable.

When we allow personal devotion to find expression in formal religion and formal religion in personal devotion; where the tradition of men and the tradition of women inform the practice of both, then some kind of balance is restored. Where faith and religious practice are not in relationship with each other, where what we do in church does not have anything to do with how we communicate and live outside church, people will clear out and do their own thing as a way of finding and celebrating meaning. The spread of alternative forms of spirituality is a reminder of the extent to which nature abhors a vacuum. The possibilities are endless, 'tarot cards and spirituality' being one of those most recently in vogue. I gazed idly at the view from Glastonbury Tor and heard a young woman of twenty or so, out for a walk with a group of handicapped people and looking for all the world like a L'Arche helper, say of a radio mast high on the Mendips opposite, 'Wouldn't it be great to put a Satanist flag on that?'

On the other hand, where religious practice is removed from personal faith even so-called believing people treat the Church as some kind of possession which is theirs to have and to hold, and indeed to manipulate. Where the Church is referred to as 'she', alarm bells should go off in our heads. 'She' can very easily be possessed or manipulated and a male cult expresses a male culture; patriarchal dominance is pervasive stuff.

The kind of faith development I am envisaging here seeks expression in religious practice, whether in personal prayer or in celebration in common. It is the faith development of believing people, people who genuinely believe that we are the Church, people who cannot bring themselves to call the Church 'she' or 'her' as though it were some kind of submissive possession, an archetype like their car or their boat. People whose desire to form Christian faith community is genuine, will necessarily want to be informed and enriched by the tradition, even as we contribute to this tradition by giving it fresh form and force in our own lives. Both the cult (or expression of our search for meaning) and the culture (or frame of reference within which we allow ourselves to search) can be enriched when informed by people who are free to find themselves as women and men before God.

What matters in all of this is the action of God; a God who does not want to be reduced to magic, to some sort of shot in the arm we receive from time to time and which works automatically with neither our co-operation nor our consent. Jesus said, 'No one can come to me unless the Father draws him; no one can come to me unless the Father draws her' (John 6.44), yet there is all the difference in the world between this gentle drawing action of God and some of the bullying we do in the name of organized religion. Drawing takes time; it has to do with attitudes and experience rather than pressure or force. Drawing elicits free choosing of God and God's ways and a level of commitment which touches us at the deepest levels of our being. People of faith will form communities of faith; such people are becoming Church nowadays as never before. For this God does not want us all to be into isolated private faith either, hyped up on private experience to the exclusion of all else, including other people. The community – however we define it – is the context in which we are invited to experience the saving call of God and to live it out.

The spirituality of all the baptized

Perhaps for this reason we are seeing the emergence of such interest in what is called 'lay spirituality' or, more usefully, the 'spirituality of all the baptized'. The personal faith of people who freely choose to respond to the drawing of God has all the characteristics of growth and movement and life that are the mark of the Spirit at work forming and fashioning the world.

This growth and movement and life lead us to discover ways of finding God in the world of our everyday living, and in particular to reappraise a culture and cult that ignore the identity and experience of half the human family. Christian living is being reconceived where we are learning to value ourselves as women – both for who we are and for what we do. Holy women are being raised up in our midst and being rediscovered in our collective Christian story.

Traditionally, the way women grow to God has of necessity been lay or non-ordained. For this reason, because this experience can speak to the way in which so many people are looking for God at the moment, it would seem important to try to see what this in fact means. Women's faith development is thereby freed from some of the sentiment which emerges when people stereotype women's emotional responses, or project aspects of their own unowned or disowned feelings onto others. We are also able to say that we envisage moral development differently, too, and that the great male goal of autonomy is not necessarily the one towards which we are moving.

If women's spirituality is different to men's, I am suggesting that some of the reasons for this are cultural: our experience is different to that of men, particularly ordained men, and so our faith response will necessarily have a different starting-point. Some of the reasons will be even deeper than that, however, and are to do with the fact that women in any case grow differently. We are subject to different natural rhythms and these will influence the way in which we come to seek and find God, both as individuals and as community. Where a woman says 'I believe', or where God is named as 'she', a certain kind of statement is being made. Any analysis of this has to take account of both our cultural and our psychological self-perception, and show a way forward that can free people in general and women in particular from false images of adult human existence.

The patterns of faith response have been usefully analysed by the American sociologist of religion, James Fowler. His ideas are of interest on two counts. One is his presentation of the various 'myths of becoming', which uncovers some of the assumptions behind ideas to do with identity and experience as discussed in the first chapter of this book. The person who is the subject of the verb 'I believe' has various ways in which to grow as a believer; in Fowler's words, there are various myths with which to wrestle as we grow towards adult human identity.

Traditionally, the Churches have presented us with the 'self-denial myth', the model of Christian virtue and progress in faith whereby everything one thinks and does and is has to be subjected to the acid test of 'if it hurts, it must be good for me'. Any one of us can think of horror stories from our past where this message was put across as hard-core gospel spirituality and the only way to God was the 'cling-to-the-rock-and-bleed' version of discipleship. This forms a terrible travesty of the great call at the heart of Christian living, the call to love and to let it be God who raises and exalts rather than ourselves. Most of the books written by people who have left the religion of their childhood or left the religious life have variant versions of the story of the child who went up to make her First Communion with a safety pin planted firmly through both her veil and her left ear by some distracted nun. The lives of the saints are littered with stories of people who had alarming ideas of how best to please God, women and men who went for the hard option before learning that there is more grace in receiving than in giving, that growth to God is not a marathon.

The opposing myth is that presented by the culture in which most of us are living nowadays. This is the myth of total 'self-realization', or 'big is beautiful/more is even better'. Every single one of us is tied into the system whereby this myth has taken hold of the popular, even the Christian, imagination. I find that the Churches do people a disservice when Christian leaders berate the secular consumer world in which we all live and then go home to enjoy a nice supper cooked by nuns or by their wives, while the rest of us are just left feeling guilty. Some of their language about social spirituality is just too glib. I was touched to see a nice young Jesuit novice wearing a T-shirt which read 'Jesuits for Justice', teased him a little – because all novices feel pretty near the bottom of the pack – by saying I would change the wording to 'Justice for Jesuits'. But then I entered a much more complicated conversation. I gave him and his fellow novices a morning's session on the place of women in the Church and ended it by referring to the T-shirt once more. A good slogan, I suggested, would be one which read, 'Jesuits for Women'.

The flip side of this, I am only too aware, is one in which men expect women to be for them. Far too much emotional laundry is already done by women for celibate men and by women religious in particular. Of far more value would be a pooling of ideas about how to live in Christian ways in a world in which everything seems to be up for grabs and the strong, arrogant and purposeful inherit the earth. What kind of a God gives us this world, the power and creativity to do good things with it, to become high-tech super-stars, even in the privacy of our own kitchens and courtesy of Magimix? Is it really a God who hates the world and is anxious that we turn our backs upon it as soon as possible, or is there something more Christian to be said about this world and living within it in faith-filled ways? Is it a God who expects the oppressed to free the oppressors or who empowers the oppressors to seek for change themselves?

What does the life of Jesus have to say to questions such as these? Is his God God the giver or God the taker-away? Is his God a God who loves the world and joins in with the human story, or a God who sits in heaven with his back turned firmly against us. Both the myth of self-denial and the myth of self-fulfilment at any price generate further myths which uncover our deepest and most unreflected attitudes, and so reveal our hidden images of God. And yet the God in whose name we have been called to practice unchristian forms of denial is the God who, in the words of Isaiah, calls us 'beloved', 'cherished', 'carved on the palm of his hand' (Isa. 49.16), and whom Hosea names as the God who 'leads us with leading-reins of love' (Hos. 11.4) and with a mother's compassion. God the seamstress who has knit our world together and who nurtures and preserves us within it seeks neither that we annihilate ourselves in her name, nor that we set ourselves up as tyrants of the material order, more keen to possess than to pass on, to master than to contemplate the mysteries of her gift. This God is the God who liberates and frees us from false images of Christian living. She is God the sharer.

For the Christian way is neither to cling to myths of self-denial nor to set up total self-realization as the ultimate object of the Christian life. Rather, in *self-acceptance* do we have some sort of way forward. The call of the gospel is a call to follow Jesus, the cross each of us is asked to bear is the cross of self-acceptance, and this we have to take up daily, in everyday situations and everyday relationships. It follows that self-knowledge and a sense of self-worth are essential to our faith development. For the self whom we are asked to accept is the true self made in God's image and likeness. It is only painful to accept this self when we refuse to believe in our own glory.

And this is where I part company with Fowler's analysis, or

rather where I think there is a further comment to be made. The burden of the tradition is such that as women we have additional work to do in appropriating ourselves as known and loved by God. Both the self-denial myth and the self-fulfilment myth have wrought havoc for our spiritual development. The double edge of both has been used against us – and often in the name of religion. The self-denial myth produced generations of women who could let others walk all over them; the self-fulfilment myth a generation who are doomed to become mannequins at the mercy of the expectations of others rather than persons in any human or alive sense of the word.

How are people, how are women in particular, to answer the gospel call and to grow in self-acceptance? James Fowler has elsewhere outlined a model for the faith development of young people and adults. His major work, *Stages of Faith*, describes the way we all come to adult faith. He is concerned to show the way in which we journey from being able to say 'I', to 'I believe', to 'I believe in God'. In its early stages faith is promoted where significant adults – parents initially, then teachers – share the ways in which they make sense of the world. After this the peer group takes over; we learn our attitudes from our friends. The way we dress, what we eat, the way in which we speak and even what we talk about are, in a certain sense, determined by the group to which we belong. The human need to belong expresses itself by the ease with which we accept the conventions of 'the group'. Many people remain in this stage for the whole of their lives, and seek and find God very helpfully in these ways. The capacity for belief which we all have is totally fulfilled by a wholehearted, generous acceptance of conventions and norms set out, for instance, by the Church, the parish, the religious Congregation or whatever.

Fowler does envisage further development, however. He goes on to describe other stages of faith where the individual goes beyond the group, is no longer indebted for salvation in quite the same way, and relies on God alone for every gift and every insight. The prophetic voice is heard most insistently from people such as these. Within each of these three sets of stages in faith development, he also describes further movement. Each attitude is internalized; people first imitate and then appropriate. In plain English this means that they at first are influenced to believe in the way their parents or friends do or God does, and then that they choose to believe in this way. In effect, therefore, there are six stages not three. Stage one is that of very young children who copy everything they learn from their parents. Learning is the necessary way in which they discover how to survive and therefore how to enjoy the emotional strength that comes with survival. At stage two they begin freely to choose the insights or ways of proceeding that they have been taught in stage one. And so, for example, they choose not to play with fire, not to talk to strangers, not to talk or scream in church.

Older children and young adults again move from outward observance of the conventions set by the group to internal allegiance. This means that in Fowler's stage three they will have their hair cut in certain ways, wear certain shoes, stand looking bored in school assembly or set the parish alight with enthusiastic liturgy because the people who influence them have marked this up as appropriate behaviour. At stage four they will do exactly the same things, but for totally different reasons. They will be the new pacesetters in a certain sense because they are now choosing the group's style, rather than merely clinging to it for conventional reasons. Adult believers who are in stages three and four will operate in similarly conventional ways; the haircut and shoes and table conversation may be more grown up, but essentially they are adopted or chosen for reasons of convention, in order to belong. The Church or faith community or religious denomination will be similarly chosen and similarly supported – and many people come to God this way.

Nevertheless, it could be argued that the kind of faith which Fowler is describing does not bear much relationship to God. The point is that he is describing the capacity for belief rather than the quality of faith a person has. When Thérèse of Lisieux asked her sisters why some people get to heaven they illustrated their answer by putting a thimble in front of her and a glass. The thimble they filled to the brim with water, the tumbler they half filled. She could then see the difference between capacity and quality. The person who is like a thimble, the person with a small capacity for belief, is nevertheless able to make a wholehearted act of faith and love. The person whose capacity, like that of a tumbler, appears larger, may nevertheless be half-hearted and making a response of much slighter quality. Fowler's stages are descriptive not judgemental.

And God seeks us and finds us, too; God is concerned about everything we feel and do, everything we suffer and die for, the everyday ways in which we search for meaning.

The believer will necessarily be able to make this connection because for the believer every meaning comes from God. God is at the source and root of all our desires, giving us the capacity of live and to trust and to endure. Nothing is insignificant, everything is open to God's call. This, essentially, is the understanding behind Fowler's thinking, and is seen most clearly in stages five and six. The insight here is that people are able to move beyond the group, and to live more freely, out of the realization that God is all in all. At first, in stage five, this realization will be imitated or adopted because it works for objective reasons. The call will be heard from sources outside the person, even though it is a divine call. In stage six the process is one of simplification and internalization; God is experienced and heard within.

Fowler gives examples of stage six people, and here I again find myself asked questions. The 'stage six people' he cites are Gandhi and Martin Luther King: another line-up of male talent. I find myself asking, is this because there are no women in stage six? Because Fowler cannot identify them? Or for a deeper reason, that at this point his analysis falls down? This is a serious claim to make, and yet one which opens up a whole range of new ways in which to look at the question. Fowler's model after all, and essentially, is of linear development. His stages follow each other; they describe progression. They make sense because they have a two-fold logic. On the one hand they identify the sources of a person's self-image – family, others, God – and on the other they trace the pattern whereby this image is internalized.

But it could be argued that this reading does not match the experience of women. If the pattern of our growth is more of a spiral than a straight line, and movement is towards externalization or other people rather than internalization or autonomy, then suddenly a whole new model of faith development emerges. This is one which speaks more clearly to women's self-perception and so to the pastoral concern of those who work as women or with women. A pattern such as this throws an entirely different light on what is being said when, as women, we begin to trust and commit ourselves to individuals, to others and to God. This is because it highlights the central importance both of self-image and of the ability to form relationships. The self is the person who is called to grow and to nourish the growth of her whole being; this she demonstrates by then moving out towards other people. The woman who feels worthless inside and who is racked by anxiety and fear cannot feed her own development. The woman who feels loved and cherished can return time and again to her own inner resources and receive the gift of life from within. Like God the sharer she thereby feeds all her relationships and within them she grows as believing woman.

For a spiral or circular model is one that keeps going back on itself in order to feed from earlier insights and to deepen them. A spiral model is one that sees development not as progress but as process, as a way in rather than a way along. The experience of most women is that this is the way we are, this is the way in which we grow. I cannot see that faith development is going to go against this rhythm. It has surely to follow the same natural pattern as the rest of our development. The word 'natural' is a useful one because it directs our search within. It makes me for one ask, 'Yes, but does this match my own experience, and what kind of an answer does it give when I listen again to the messages that have formed so many of the scripts I have had to struggle to abandon?'

On the one hand I have heard it said that there are no differences between men and women except for those which have been given us by our culture and which therefore can be rejected. On the other I have heard equally extravagant claims based on a fundamentalist version of biology. It is not insignificant that most of the Roman Catholic Church's teaching on sex (as opposed to sexuality) was developed in the light of Thomas Aquinas' understanding. He imagined that the complete human person in embryo was contained in male sperm, that the woman was only the weaker and non-contributory partner who lodged this perfect male product for nine months. Instant babies were transferred on penetration. Male sexual pleasure could therefore be set up as the paradigm and be institutionalized in the Roman Catholic Church's formal codes of law; ethics become a way of juggling with mechanical problems rather than reflecting on the place of relationships. In a Peanuts cartoon Linus gasps with relief on hearing a theological presentation of the flood story. Charlie Brown comments, 'Sound theology has a way of doing that.' Sound biology, too, enables us to separate the unnatural from the natural, the sentimental from the familiar, the inhuman from the human – and begin to work with this.

Jesus in the Gospels is at pains to remind the woman at the well of Samaria that the source of her own life and potential for growth lies within. She has springs of living water that can nourish her time and again and to which she knows she can return. This story is one that speaks to the experience of every human being. Yet originally it was the story of a woman and her meeting with a saviour who sought to vindicate her own experience of growing and marking time. I am reminded of a prayer of confession prepared by a consultation of Methodist women ministers in Oxford and published in a collection entitled *Celebrating Women*:

> God our Creator, we come to confess that we have failed: we have not made room for sisters and brothers to be themselves; we have rejected the space you have made for us, and clung to the narrow limits imposed by false expectations; we have treated with distaste the delicate, beautiful workings of our bodies.
>
> For our failure to accept what we are, our refusal to allow our bodies to speak to our minds and our spirits, our inability to cope with being made in the image of God – Gracious and accepting God, forgive us.

Janet Morley and Hannah Ward, eds.
Celebrating Women (Movement for the Ordination of Women, and Women in Theology 1986) p. 23.

Where God the Creator is named and found within, so many of our familiar categories have to be reappraised. And so, for instance, when we hear it said that women are not as strong as men, what kind of strength is being talked about – force or endurance? Force after all belongs with linear growth; endurance with growth in depth. The one may be about movement away from other people; the other is about moving towards them. We hear it said that women are unreliable, that we cannot be depended upon to be feeling the same way each day. Are qualities of flexibility and adaptability unimportant, therefore? Circular movement is good enough for planet earth, for the moon, the seasons and the tides. Why not for people, too? Why does everything have to be thought of in terms of horizons and goals and objects? What is the matter with the rhythms of nature? Time is more than *chronos*, the straight accumulation of one day upon another. Time is about development, too, and lived out in our experience of any growing process. Men can live time in this way just as well as women, but because *chronos* has been such a tyrant for so long, other patterns have been submerged.

Where women's identity is allowed to be distinctive, where women's experience of development is vindicated as a legitimate way to God, this way is made accessible to more people, including those men who are learning to recognize and nurture the divine image as an image of wholeness. The developing girl, the developing woman, the woman who can bear children (including the sexual celibate), the older woman, each of these is coming to God in ways that can inform the spirituality of any one of us. Where the cycles we live and develop within are used creatively, a whole spirituality becomes possible, one in which the words belief, disbelief, prayer and activity have a context. The insights of someone like James Fowler are useful in that they help us to make the quantum leap of imaging other forms of development. But where we look to our own experience of growing as women his model raises as many questions as it answers. For an understanding of what this means in my own experience and that of women I know, I find that there is more thinking to be done. One pattern is that of cyclic growth, of returning to one's own inner process; the other, and this must be examined in the next chapter, is that of moving from the particular to the general, from the inside outwards.

6
On being
a Praying Woman

Models of prayer

If a spiral model of growth can give further insights into the specific quality of women's spirituality and so speak to some of the questions raised in the first chapter of this book, so, too, an understanding of how we move outwards from the centre can open up the whole area of faith response in prayer as outlined in the second chapter. Reflective living helps us to reclaim our experience and to hear the call of God within the events and above all within the relationships of the everyday. It offers us an integrating spirituality, one that seeks to make sense of the whole of our reality not just of part of it, so that everything we do is done within the context of our life of faith, and becomes a kind of prayer or way of praying.

Within this understanding, how do women in particular grow as praying people? How do we learn to live in reflective ways? Initially I can best answer this question in terms of my own experience. I find that whereas, when I was a child, I used to pray only with words sanctioned for use by my Church, now I pray in all sorts of ways including without words. When I was a child I had to be in church or before the altar set up in my bedroom in order to pray, and I thought praying meant saying prayers. Now I pray anywhere; I was going to say everywhere – because I understand prayer differently. The altar in the bedroom is significant, however, because I also spent long hours playing a game called 'Being an Altar Boy', and spent a lot of energy cutting up pretend hosts out of white drawing paper. Somehow, and rather dimly, I was beginning to learn that prayer can also be a way of doing other things, too. At the time I obviously thought that those things had to be holy things, but at least the insight was taking shape. In general I am describing movement into unity and harmony; contexts that come closer and closer to the still room off the kitchen in the house where I was brought up in Somerset, rather than to the ornate Oratory church in Birmingham where my journey began. This is what I mean by movement from the inside outwards, in that the sources that feed one's being as a praying women are found within and gradually inform everything one is and does.

I have a written record of those early years in the form of the book I prepared for my First Communion. I was seven years old when I wrote: 'Dear God, I am sorry I have done big or little sinners. I will not do them agin, I hope.' The note of realism in that final interjection reminds me that while I was pious, I was not innocent. 'Dear God I am glad you are going to comentomysole. When I have made my 1 communion I will get more grace.' Words like grace and sin and soul abound; grace being something I should collect, sin something I should avoid. They are interspersed with topical references such as: 'Dear God please bless the pope and make him a well man.' (This was 1954 and Pius XII was seriously ill.)

In 1960 I wrote another prayer book, as it were *The Prayers of Lavinia Byrne aged 13¾*. What appals me as I read them now is that the vocabulary I used in personal prayer was still so clearly about sin and fear. And so I wrote: 'Forgive me my sins O Lord. I want to be good and holy, not sinful and bad.' My experience was something that I sought to avoid. The honesty of an Adrian Mole is light years away. 'Give me complete new life so that I may always love you and want to serve you as is your most holy will.' 'You were always good. You never disobeyed. You did not grumble or argue. Since you made it Lord, your world has become a horrible place full of sin. Nothing is good unless it comes from you.' The imagery is worrying, too: about lambs and immolation and sacrifice, or the soul and separation, sin and chastisement.

Movement came only when I started to pray with Scripture and to use the Bible as a way to come to God. Then I discovered the Jesus of history and began to reflect slowly, using the words of the psalms in particular and the Gospel stories. I liked the words I found and liked listening to the voice of Jesus. Only in time did I begin to pray the Scriptures with my imagination, and this in turn led to something of a breakthrough. Instead of the text being 'out there', or back there in history, I came to it as someone with my own story and found that the contexts in which I imagined Jesus were contemporary scenes, those of my everyday life. The concerns I took to him were real concerns, those of my everyday relationships.

Once this began to be the case the next stage was obvious. The Jesus who came to me when I imagined myself into Gospel scenes was a Jesus who forgave me and offered me rest. All the knots into which my religious formation had tied me, all the ways in which I had misread the good and fallen for the bad, all the signals about perfection and pleasing God were undone, taken away from me, removed. I could live openly and honestly with God, even when I lost my nerve and did not believe in the freedom I was being given. I should add that a retreat, and a long one at that, was the context within which this understanding became real for me. Since that time I have received spiritual direction as a regular way of trying to live out of this experience and to let it inform my daily living.

Some time after this retreat I found regular opportunities for an activity which in itself demands only sixty per cent of my full attention, a very rhythmic activity with its own space and silence and its own lessons. I could be talking about knitting or weaving or using rosary beads but in fact I am talking about bicycling. Beyond the level of conscious activity there is another level of awareness where I have greater access to my feelings, memory and imagination. When I bicycle home at the end of each day I have time to listen to these reflectively and to hear the call of God who speaks to me within. I begin to notice patterns and to make connections. I begin to see analogies between what I find inside and the world outside. I begin to be more attentive to sight and sound and smell, to the light and the dark, the heat and the cold, the sun and the rain. I have found a harmony I had not known before, between foot and pedal, hand and eye certainly, but also between inside and outside. This harmony is offered to me as a way of living that is God-centred, and so a new image of prayer.

This harmony is what I also experience in times of more formal personal prayer. There is so little to say about it because it is just there. How I feed this prayer is another matter and one which does need some kind of comment. There are certain places that are helpful to me. Not places that qualify for the name holy as it is ordinarily used, but places that are holy to me. A place in the north of France, half in the country and half beside the sea. A place where I know I have met God and will meet God again. There are people who are important as well, people who restore my sense of being loved and being able to love; and so holy people whom God has given me. There are times of day that suit and others that do not. There are passages from the Scriptures, familiar verses and scenes and those which I turn up by chance. And so I let my memory feed this prayer, because my memory is full of moments when I have felt God at work in my life or been moved by what I have read and remembered, heard and retained. My memory is saturated with Christian experience, my own and that of the tradition. There have been times in my life when certain practices have been important to me, such as saying the Divine Office of the Church. And always as backdrop to my moods and certainties, there is the liturgical year and everything it is doing to inform my sense of living in terms of the Christian mysteries.

What I am describing here is how one very ordinary woman of forty prays. What I find moving is that this is the experience of so many of the women I know and – in particular – that the life situations of many of them are totally unlike my own. They will describe the road differently, but their journey has taught them to listen to what is within and learn how to live out of this.

I had a lovely dream: I was with an old woman who had made a jacket and it was the most beautiful thing I have ever seen, different layers of fabric and lace, and deep rich colours changing and blending, and subtle patterns. She said she would show me how to make one and I was so excited. I think she is God telling me we can make my life together and it will be beautiful and deep and rich. She's not just doing to drop it into my lap, we have to make it together. So I cry but I am given hope.

Letter from Louisa Blair, Ignatius Farm Community, Guelph, Ontario, 25 July 1987

It is a journey out of fear into love; a journey away from the imagery of sacrifice and oblation, through sentiment to commitment; a journey which becomes increasingly simple and yet which unifies and integrates. The experience is one of relationship but nevertheless of the complete otherness of a God who envelopes and enfolds and who is more cloud and space than image and word.

The common experience is that as children we were taught 'the correct order of words' by which the believing community addresses God. These become less adequate as we grow older, particularly when the language in which they are written is sexist, the experience they value is exclusive, the God they propose so exclusively male. The discovery of variety is an important way forward, and with it the realization that time spent in silence with God is as much prayer as time spent repeating the words Jesus first taught his disciples when they asked for something to go on as they began to pray. Spending time contemplating the presence of God in the market-place is as much prayer as dwelling prayerfully on the words of Scripture. After all there are many ways of praying, each more or less valid for the context within which we are in fact coming to God.

If 'saying prayers' is set up as the only way of praying, however, liturgical prayer becomes a tyranny, for personal prayer, too, begins to be about sound rather than silence; further words are generated – as in prayers of intercession – and this form of praying is set up as an idol rather than as one model among many. The way of praying that is appropriate to one way of life, or one moment in one's own life, can too easily become a millstone. The praying person is a free person, someone who is free to choose what works, and to abandon what does not. So no form of prayer is deemed superior; all that matters is whether it is right for the moment. An objective test of this rightness might be to ask whether this is a prayer that leads me to live out of my centre and to integrate what I find there with what I find outside. Does it lead outwards towards others or inwards towards myself? Is it prayer that isolates me from my experience or which calls me to reflect upon this experience so that I can hear the next call of God within this reflection?

The place of reflection

For God both made and likes the human condition; Jesus chose it as his way of coming to the Father; the Spirit broods over our world. Human experience has an absolute value, whether at the time it feels good or feels bad. Any other way of looking at our reality, any way which divides our story into what is holy and therefore somehow acceptable to God and what is unholy and therefore definitely not, forces us to compartmentalize our lives. Each of us can think of instances of our own pain, of our own pleasure, and ask whether this is our understanding or whether we in fact work out of a divided understanding. Do I honestly believe that God is interested in my life, or not? In order for intercessory prayer to be real, does its object have to be something big like the nuclear threat or world poverty, or can I talk about what is really worrying me – the real anxieties I feel about getting to the shops or finding a parking space, let alone my relationships with the people with whom I live, my everyday anxieties and pleasures?

In order for prayer to be real it has to be about what is real to me. Where we begin to take experience seriously we are committed to praying in ways that commit us to be serious about our own situation and our own relationships. This means that experience on its own is not enough, for it to be integrated and lived before God such experience has to be relived in faith. I am reminded of Gerard Manley Hopkins' line in *The Wreck of the Deutschland*, 'Over again I feel thy finger and find thee'. For life to be lived in faith-filled ways, what is necessary is to reflect upon God's touch, to be sensitive and aware at all times.

Other kinds of prayer can be a kind of cop-out. It is very easy to pray for an end to world conflict and then waltz out and have a blinding row. It is very easy to pray for an end to world starvation and then open up a packet of convenience food that has been prepared at the expense of other people's agriculture and economy. Neither is a particularly Christian thing to do. Where we do pray for things, the ideal, of course, would be to use prayers that bring together both our own needs and those of the wider world: to pray for an end to the hostility that eats away at our own hearts in the confidence that the world will gradually become a more peaceful place thereby; to pray for the concern to take food and the whole business of feeding people seriously, in the certainty that this will ultimately make a difference to the way in which resources are distributed; to pray for the courage to speak out against injustice.

In church one hears prayers of intercession which let the Christian community off every hook imaginable. Firstly there are those which divide experience: 'Set the peace of heaven in our hearts, Lord, so that we may pass unscathed through this vale of tears and come to your throne untroubled by the cares and preoccupations of this present life.' Then there are those which disengage us even from the one or two realities we do admit:

'Lord, we pray for the handicapped (the unemployed/sick/desti-
tute, etc.) that they may be courageous in accepting what is
happening to them.' Even through the parody, these are recognizable sentiments one has heard voiced from the sanctuary. Such
prayers can so easily be rewritten: 'Set the peace of heaven in our
hearts so that we may work with your confidence when we
undertake to help the handicapped and the sick. Help us to learn
from their courage and give us some of their patience.' The same
applies with the little prayers we make about finding parking
spaces or things we have lost, about passing exams and hoping for
good weather and so on; either we can ask God to work magic on
our behalf or we can call on God, asking for help to look at our
world with the eyes of faith.

Where we are committed to sharing this vision of God we will
find that we are unable to look on the human story through
jaundiced eyes because God does not have the same problem with
human experience that we seem to have. Every situation is open to
be talked through in prayerful ways and, even better than that,
every situation is there to be reflected over even as we are living
through it. Paul (not a favourite writer with the feminist sister-
hood) exhorted the Christian community to pray at all times, to
pray without ceasing. This does not mean that we have to be saying
prayers all the time. J D. Salinger parodied the strange effect this
can have on someone's life in his novel *Franny and Zooey*. His
young heroine ended up as a zombie. The praying person is not
someone who is numbed and de-sensitized; if anything, the
praying person is committed to extraordinary sensitivity, to
constant awareness. The praying person is in a conscious relationship with God.

What does this mean in reality? A God who is as familiar as the
air we breathe is given to us on every breath. A God who is at play
in the world is there in our every action. A God who is love is there
in all our loving. By awareness we advert to this presence, we do
not create it. Rather we let it speak to us and touch us at every
moment. So how do we do this? How do we love in any case? The
feelings we have when we fall in love give us a level of tenderness
and sensitivity that are absent from most relationships, even those
we enjoy with our closest friends. Our reactions are no longer
totally our own, there is a sense in which they are shared because
we begin to identify with the reactions of the person loved. What

would he make of this? What would she make of this? We put on the mind of the person we love and begin to see the world through eyes other than our own.

More than this, we long to share our day with that person, to talk through its ups and downs, to grow together through the ordinary experiences of daily living. This gives a major insight, I believe, into what is meant by becoming a praying person. We share both the storyline of what we have lived through with the person we love and our reactions to it. Our sentences begin, 'I felt really happy/really annoyed today', 'I found myself longing to do so and so', 'I needed to see you, to talk to you'. What we share with people we love is our emotional life. And where we begin to be reflective people before God, we begin to be free to share in the same way, too.

God knows the storyline of our day in all its detail and how it fits in with the rest of the human story, the story of the people around us. If we are to get to know God better, the place to hear best will be within our own emotional reactions to this story, within our feelings. In this way we can seek and find God in all things and enjoy the freedom to live every event and every relationship as praying people. If God really is present in all things, absent from none, this is not some kind of physical presence, a localizing of God in some physical sense. If that were the case we would be back to the spirituality which condemned people to pursue what Julian Huxley called 'the fading smile of a cosmic Cheshire Cat'. And in any case, how can God's presence be defended in some of the uglier aspects of our world? How can God be present in a nuclear warhead, for instance? One understanding is that God is present in our reactions to these things, and therefore that we can both seek and find God in our feelings. The fear I feel when faced with danger, the anger when faced with injustice, the joy when surprised by friendship, pleasure in celebration, grief at sickness and death are all natural, human ways in which God is communicating with me and inviting me to listen and to answer.

This list necessarily contains some emotions we ordinarily would call negative. Fear and anger and grief are natural, certainly, but are they really ways in which God is touching my life? Should emotions such as these really be allowed to darken my way to God? Surely nice peaceful emotions are appropriate and not these negative ones? God makes the human heart and gives us the capacity to have these feelings. More then that, we *should* feel fear and outrage at injustice, we *should* mind terribly that people die. The ability to have these feelings is part of the way in which we grow and become more human. Some of what we do with these feelings may indeed be less than human, however, and perhaps sensitivity here is the best way of all of becoming aware of God and of the divine call. People who do not admit that they have feelings cut themselves off from the possibility of coming to God through the natural and the human, through the ordinary fabric of everyday life. People who do own their feelings open up the possibility of growing to God in this way.

What I am suggesting is that it is not enough simply to have feelings. A praying person will work with these feelings and listen to the God who speaks through them. A praying person is able to journey to God in natural, human ways thereby. For with reflection it becomes possible to see where these feelings come from and more importantly where they are going to lead us. We become more experienced in remembering the ways in which we have made good or bad choices in the past as a result of comparable feelings. We become altogether wiser, people who are better able to hear and to recognize what God is saying to us and how we can live out of what we hear.

This way of coming to God is a hard way because it means taking on a great deal of responsibility for how one lives. There are no easy answers, no formulae one can trot out because they have universal application. Each day will make its own demands and give its own rewards. And so each day must contain space in which to reflect. Some people do their best reflecting at the hairdressers; others in the bath. So how does one set about finding comparable patches of time and space in a busy day? They present themselves in such improbable ways, because of course they do exist, only we do not always identify them too easily. A lot of people hate ironing because it seems mindless, or washing up for the same reason. Yet arguably both these activities provide an ideal opportunity to make contact with one's feelings precisely because they are mechanical tasks and so only relatively demanding. They also provide analogies. I can now make lots of parallels between the experience of bicycling and the experience of living. Both are chequered by uphills and downhills, moments when I know the way and moments when I am lost. Both are about movement, about using energy sensibly, about counting on help from other people and about knowing when to rest. When I am sensitive to these analogies, then I become a more reflective person in all I am and do.

There are other ways in which this kind of contact with God in the familiar and the everyday can be sustained and fed. What nourishes any relationship? Time spent with the person certainly, but also a sharing of interests and of friends. Time spent alone reflecting, time spent alone watching and listening to Jesus in the pages of the Gospels, time spent alone in the presence of God who is creator and sanctifier will be creative, sanctifying time. But equally time spent with people and time spent within the local faith community of one's own family or friends is there to be discovered as Godtime. If I believe that God is actively interested and engaged in my world I will find God there and not have to go elsewhere. Moreover the God I find is likely to prove to be the nurse and mother (Num. 11.12; Isa. 46.3), the midwife (Ps. 22.9) and homemaker (Luke 15.8–10) of Scripture, the one who shares my concern with the world and the people I love.

What kind of path will a praying woman follow as she journeys in this way? I have suggested already that there are appropriate ways in which the developing girl, the developing woman, will grow to God once her identity as woman is owned. But what will this really mean as women pray their way into discipleship? How will the Christian pattern be lived out in their lives? How will any Christbearing woman grow as a praying woman?

The praying woman

Traditional Christian spirituality has not always been particularly helpful to women because all too often it has proposed that most sophisticated of virtues, humility, to those who are not yet ready to deal with it. Women approach all power, all strength, all authority from a position of weakness. Not because we are weak and feeble people but because we have been treated as such for centuries. The first Christian task is to come to full, adult stature as people whom God has made and whom God finds good. In this way we come to glory.

The Gospels present us with a Jesus who comes to God this way, a Jesus who 'grows in wisdom and grace and in favour with God and other people' (Luke 2.52). The first half of the Gospels presents us with a Jesus who is alive and active, who is the subject of every verb. He reaches out his hand to touch people, he eats and drinks with them, he walks and talks, he loves and feels angry, he notices and comments, he observes and heals. Only at the end of the story does he become the person to whom things are done; then is he arrested and led and stripped and crucified and his life is taken from him. The model of Christian living we have here is one of development and fulfilment, of coming to the fulness of life, even if one's capacity for fulness is as small as that of a thimble. The message is that each of us can find the abundance that is 'life in all its fulness' (John 10.10), and pray out of this understanding.

And just in case that were not clear enough, we have in the Gospels that remarkable story about the freeing of two women to present us with a living diptych of Jesus' concern with our condition. He actively intervenes in the lives of Jairus' young daughter and the unnamed woman with the haemorrhage, two women who are groaning under their condition as victims of a system that seeks to destroy them. This system had got itself in the way of ordinary human and life-enhancing relationships; and moreover, it had done this in the name of religion. The Jewish religious Law forbade girls access to adult identity in the synagogue and menstruating women access to the market-place, the well, the social life of the community. Jairus' son had no such problems. At the age of twelve he could be bar mitzvah'd, made an adult member of the community, and join the quorum of ten males required by the Law for valid worship in the synagogue (the presence of praying women being beside the point). At the age of twelve he would become adult in the eyes of the community, and this honour would be accorded publicly to him. Living out this condition might present problems and be a painful experience. Jesus himself at twelve years old had to grope about to find out what to do and how. He had to listen and to ask questions of the elders, to seek his Father's will and test his relationships within the family. My point, however, is that boy children as they moved into adolescence received a form of public recognition which had heavy religious overtones. God's approval was conveyed to them in a recognizable package. Girl children had no comparable affirmation.

Jairus' daughter must have had her own name as well. Part of her problem, one assumes, was that the Law had her future in tight knots. Jairus himself was no doubt the man of faith and quality Jesus found him to be. Mrs Jairus is one of the missing figures of Scripture. For as long as the child had been alive, the sort of future possible to her is that parodied by the condition of the other woman who shares her story. Not only does adolescence hold natural fear for her because it is doing strange things to her body, but as well she looks around her and sees society punishing women like her in the name of religion. In these circumstances is there any point in growing up, in living at all for that matter? Jesus' life-giving word restores an identity to her. He calls her what she feels herself to be and promises her something great: 'Little girl, I say to you arise' (Luke 8.54). These words constitute a call to adult life which is in no way bound to or by the demands of the Law, a call which she can answer directly without the intervention of anyone but a Jesus who saves her from the Law.

Her answer – and the answer given by the woman with the haemorrhage – is to move forward confidently into adult life as someone fully alive. The fact that each is woman is not something to be ashamed of but something to be rejoiced in. Once this identity is owned then all the experience of being woman can be lived out before God. There is no hierarchy in Jesus' scheme of things. Neither identity nor experience is deemed to be superior; each is valid, each is a legitimate way of coming before God. The woman disciple can pray as freely out of her experience as the male disciple out of his; the young person as freely as the older person.

What will this mean in practice? I have intimated that the movement envisaged by Christian formation is identified by the word humility. John the Baptist prayed that Jesus might be greater, that he might be less. The Christian disciple is the one who leans on Jesus' heart and stands beneath his cross. The grain of wheat falling into the ground must die for any new life to be brought forth. Christianity reads failure and sickness and pain and grief anew, but likewise Christianity reads living and growing and sharing anew. The grain of wheat is an object, while the consenting human person is capable of making a personal response, of self-offering. God is not a whimsical tyrant who wants people to be humiliated. God calls us to justice and integrity, to life, and life in all its fulness. This is the God whom we hear saying, 'I will give you the treasures of darkness, riches stored in secret places, so that you may know that I am the Lord, the God of Israel, who calls you by name' (Isa. 45.3). The disciple who leans against the breast of Jesus is answering the call of love, being where Jesus is and content to rest there, learning the treasures of darkness with him.

The disciple who leans against the breast of Jesus is a person who feels at home with her God because she has heard and lived through the total experience of discipleship. She has not just arrived out of the sky and ended up instantaneously in the best seat. Rather, hers is a living out of the incarnation; she knows the weak God who comes as baby and infant, she knows the growing God who finds human ways of coming to holiness, who chooses friends and companions for the task. She has laboured through the heat of the day, has grown intimate with the ways of the Father who is also Mother, and knows the mind of Jesus. She is a woman of stature, a woman in whom the Spirit is at work. Empowered by the gospel this disciple will go even to Calvary, because she has understood that at Calvary love triumphs over fear; relationships triumph over autonomy. Jesus dies as the final victim demanded by the law of fear, the law of holocaust and sacrifice. His is the God who gives life not the God who takes it away, and at Calvary this God is given to the world upon the dying breath of Jesus. The woman who prays out of this understanding of herself as disciple is not going to be led astray by false, unchristian images of self-immolation. Moreover she will be charged to carry the news of the resurrection into the world and so become apostle.

To come to God in this way we need open hands and a loving heart, the ability to receive and the desire to give, but above all the courage and confidence to stay with what we have learnt in prayer. Women have too easily in the past been asked to sacrifice themselves upon the altar of a God misread, a God imaged as tyrant rather than a God imaged as life-giver and nurturer, as parent and as friend. Behind the sacrifices asked of us in the name of religion lay too much social convention and conditioning; woman the queen of shining floors has man the king of the universe walk all over her far too easily. When any of us makes the Christian gesture of offering ourselves in love to diminishment and weakness, we can do so only at the request of God. For God alone can give the treasures of darkness, God alone can call us beyond these into eternal life. Other calls to diminishment are the work of that Satan who asked Jesus to throw himself off the side of the Temple, to make a heroic gesture in the name of religion, isolate himself and, thereby, to test God.

For this reason above all, sensitivity to the call of God is of paramount importance. Only a person who is sensitive in everyday life, reflective and aware of the movement of God within the detail of the real is going to hear the gospel call in the events of life. A praying person is not going to miss the cues. Moreover a praying woman lives within cycles of growth and diminishment which, if anything, are going to help her to hear and read aright when God's call to failure and sickness, to pain and grief, does come. For the redeeming God who begins each cycle afresh, who offers new life against all the odds, is familiar and known by name. Where women share in the incarnation and the public life of Jesus, we can safely share in the mysteries of his passion, death and resurrection. In prayer we learn ourselves as disciples of this Jesus, as daughters of a God who sets us free, as enfolded by the Spirit in an embrace that is more tender than passionate.

In this way our experience of the particular enables us to live with the general. Our knowledge from within, from that place we call the heart but which in reality is the body, can lead us to make applications which have some sort of exterior validity. This movement from the inside outwards is a resource which is going to give a special flavour to the Christian service of praying women in so far as it represents a commitment to relationships. All that is needed is to examine and, ideally, to demythologize certain images of Christian ministry as performed by women and to see how women carry the news of the resurrection into the world.

7
On being Woman in the World

Images of woman

'Into the room she came, a big woman – not at all your classical nun
. . .' 'When I was little I thought I ought to be a nun, but then I
met Peter so I settled for him.' 'I've seen *The Sound of Music*
twenty-seven times.' Behind chance remarks such as these – and
each of us could supply others – lie all sorts of assumptions which I
enjoy summarizing in terms of the song title from *The Sound of
Music*: 'Climb every Mountain'. However, to get the full effect it
has to be turned into a question and said on a note of rising panic:
'Climb *every* mountain?' Is our image of Christian service one of
striving and straining? Is our underlying view that nuns have it
made and that the rest of us are somehow second-best or lesser
citizens in the great race Godwards? Moreover, in our heart of
hearts do we have a romantic image of nuns, as legless beings only
partly of this world?

Both the theology, which assumes that God lives on top of a
mountain, and the spirituality, which assumes that one has to keep
going up mountains in order to find God, are relics of a former way
of thinking which does a disservice to our understanding of how
we may try to come to God as women engaged in Christian
ministry, and how we bring the news of the resurrection into the
world. The kind of Christian ministry I am talking about is that
described in chapter three: the service of people who believe they
may seek and find God within the relationships and situations of
their everyday lives; people whose desire it is to reclaim and
declericalize this ministry, so that its place in any faith response
makes better sense of the idea of vocation and the universal call to

holiness of all the baptized.

In the case of women, understanding vocation is especially important because the serving face of the Church has not only been clericalized but also over-identified with one particular group of people: the nuns. Neither the vocation of nuns nor the vocation of lay people has emerged unscathed; what it means to be as Christian woman and to do as Christian woman has been hopelessly sentimentalized; Christian marriage, the single state and the religious life have been set up in opposition to each other rather than appreciated as distinct and totally complementary ways of living a faith-filled life in service of the world.

The first thing to try to salvage is the idea of vocation as both call and response. The call may be one (the one call we all receive to be human and holy and so to live out what we are baptized to be), but there are many different ways of answering this call. There must be different ways otherwise we would all be clones of each other. The person who goes into a convent does not have a superior call, the person who marries an inferior one; they both have an identical call. The voice of God is one; God's call alone gives us our true name. 'Thou, O Lord, art is the midst of us, and we are called by thy name; leave us not' (Jer. 14.9b). As different human beings we will have different ways of responding to God, but these in turn do not fragment the call. They merely vindicate the generosity of God in making us different and allowing us the freedom to experience discipleship in different ways. The key word is freedom. Where we give people the freedom to see that they have many different ways of answering God's one call, they are freed from the tyranny of imagining that there is a hierarchy of vocation. This is the tyranny we used to call 'having a vocation' – as though everyone else did not and as though it were like the mumps at that. I well remember my mother leaning across the table confidentially and saying in a quiet voice: 'Have you heard Lavinia's news?' as though I were ill or something.

This freedom to be different from each other and yet to live a faith-filled life means that we can look in reflective ways at our understandings of what it is to be an adult Christian woman who is committed to service. It means that we can look at our own identity and experience and learn their lessons without being asked to judge them. There are lots of images circulating in the popular understanding at the moment, and if I choose to analyse them in terms of nuns this reflects nothing more than my own interests and experience. I do, however, believe that much of what can be said about this particular group of women has general application to the condition of all Christbearing women. I should add that I have also found that what men say about nuns is most revealing as an indication of what they really think of all women.

My interest in the question was first raised when I was asked to speak about nuns in the university Roman Catholic chaplaincy at Cambridge. Suddenly I felt that I had had enough of doing an 'all you've ever wanted to know about nuns and never liked to ask' presentation because it struck me that this would merely perpetuate some of the myths. Since that evening I have begun to explore some of the connections that have to exist between the experience of the young women and men I was talking to and the point I was trying to make about adult Christian presence in the world. I had come across a book prepared in the 1960s by a sister in the United States, who wrote of the various images of nuns she had met in literature. These were the sentimental nun figure of Arthurian romance; the debased nun figure of satire and the mechanical or traditional ideal nun type. She had extensive references to illustrate each of these categories; a wealth of nuns, from Milton's quiet one, bent in prayer, to Chaucer's jolly, stylish one who in general was not. I found these labels helpful, found that I could add others from my own experience of literature; then I realized that they had present-day equivalents, and the hunt was on.

Friends came up with further models, and so I discovered the handless angel, the discontinued-line nun, the campaign for real nuns nun, the hunky cross nun, the ceramics and leather thong nun, the tweedy virgin, Sr Marks and Spencer (with her rich relations, Sr Jaeger and Sr Laura Ashley), the strip-tease nun, the radical nun, the silver screen nun and, for the mechanical nun, do we have the strobe nun? Once again this list contains some images that can be seen as sentimental or as debased, some that are instantly recognizable even though one may not like them particularly, and some that feel distinctly right. I am reluctant to look at them in terms of hierarchy as my central concern here is to avoid hierarchies, precisely because I am concerned with the freedom we all have to answer God's call differently.

If they were grouped more constructively, other ways of looking at this freedom might stand out more clearly. And so there is the real nun, the professional woman nun and the radical nun. Each of them can be misunderstood and parodied, so this necessarily throws up the silver screen nun, the pornographic nun and the failed wife/failed lesbian nun. Moreover each of these conceals further images of Christian service, so that there is a hidden agenda behind these apparent stereotypes. If I use the stereotypes here, it is only so that these images can be uncovered.

The real nun

The real nun is the woman who follows the monastic way of life. In itself hers is a radical choice; she lives in a convent which may or may not be enclosed and leads a life governed by one of the older rules for the religious life – that of St Benedict or St Augustine, for instance. She is what we are often thinking about when we talk of nuns; the way she has chosen is the paradigm in terms of which we are inclined to discuss all other forms of religious life. Hers is a regular day of prayer and work, her convent a place where God is known by name and served in love and freedom. The enclosure is not there to keep her in but to keep us out, and if she does come out of her cloister she is likely to wear a recognizable habit as manifestation of cloister and of her apartness. It could be argued that hers is the most mysterious of all answers to God's call because it constitutes such a distinct alternative to the way in which most of us live. I remember asking a Carmelite prioress how they were doing for vocations in her community and being delighted with her answer: 'Three people in ten years, quite enough for us.'

Because hers is a hidden vocation, it is the most easily misunderstood and the most open to parody. The silver screen phenomenon is the obvious one. When nuns are depicted in films or on television the image is all too easily romantic and sentimental. Some progress has been made: the nuns in *Agnes of God* are closer to real people than those of *The Sound of Music* or *The Nun's Story*, for instance. But nevertheless the image of convent and of religious life is still as mindless and the storyline is equally improbable. Contemplative nuns have done as much as anyone else to rethink their vocation with the mind of the present-day Church. They have done as much as anyone else to return to the sources of their vocation, to the reasoning that lay behind that retreat into the desert which characterized the first forms of religious life in the fourth century of the Church's history. The distinctive step is that of flight as a way of engaging with the forces of evil; the desert was the unconverted place where early religious could be sure that they were being truly radical. Their intention was not to run away from but to run towards God's call to be Christian and to form community. Chastity, poverty and obedience came later, as means to an end rather than as absolutes in their own right.

At its best this way of life has given the Church some of its finest women, women who have developed within their answer to God's call because theirs was a commitment to depend upon God alone for salvation and upon other women for support and companionship. This of course is what attracts the flak; we find it hard to believe that people who choose a way of life that stands in contradiction to our own understanding can develop in natural ways as human beings. Certainly their way of life is not normal, and that is why this answer is so seldom given – the monastic vocation is a rarity but this does not make it freakish, nor does it make the women who follow it freaks. The work they do ought to give us pause because it is hidden work and apparently ineffectual. In this way they have much in common with other women whose area of competence and authority is the home or the office; women whose achievement is taken for granted; women who are never thanked; women who are expected to suffer in silence and yet who find support in the companionship they enjoy with each other. They are called by God's name and pray 'Leave us not.'

The image of woman which monastic religious project can be a way in to understanding an image of woman with which a number of women are working. That is to say that they too are living by rules invented initially by men – even though in their case the names are not as hallowed as those of Augustine and Benedict. They too are trying to bring about the Kingdom of God in the everyday circumstances of furnishing and providing and cooking and cleaning and manufacturing. If they redeem the world it is by having the courage to take themselves seriously and by the quality of relationships with which they transform the home or factory or hospital or school which is their workplace and, increasingly, by their commitment to a more just and peaceful world for us all. There are as many contemplatives among them as there are in the monastic cloister, for the contemplative vocation is not limited to any one state of life.

This way of life is as open to parody and misunderstanding as is that of the monastic tradition. And so we have films in which the little wife or the little secretary are figures of fun, or sentimental figures with conventional virtues and no vices, anything but flesh and blood people with real needs and real feelings. If I describe their life as a challenge to our way of thinking, this is because these women, too, do not depend upon achievement for salvation. Their experience dictates otherwise. People rather than achievements sanctify, and God is the first saviour, the one who exalts the lowly. The mystery of coming to God in everyday ways and choosing community as the medium for experiencing this coming is one we are tempted to parody because we just do not understand it. Real nuns, real women, are engaged in forms of ministry and service that are essentially interpersonal. This vocation is apostolic because every Christian vocation is apostolic; their response, meanwhile, reminds us of the value of being the Kingdom of God in the midst of the world. 'Thou, O Lord, art in the midst of us' (cf. Zeph. 3.17).

The professional nun

In contrast to the real nun there stands the professional nun, the Marks and Sparks nun, the trained teacher or nurse or social worker nun. In fact she is not really a nun at all; the Church calls her an active apostolic religious woman and sometimes has diffi- culty with her. Is she called to service of the Church or service in the Church? Is she a person who can be pushed in to fill a gap, a form of free labour, the kind of nun who ends up making the beds in a Roman seminary because her Congregation made the mistake of calling themselves the 'Slaves of Christ'? Or is she a force to be reckoned with, a person with a valid contribution to make, a person whose training qualifies her to take initiatives and make decisions? The active apostolic sister will quite likely live in a small community, with a lifestyle that accommodates her professional commitments. She will wear clothes that suit her way of life because she is saying something about the presence of Christ in the world. His is not the shiny presence of Mount Tabor; rather his is the way of the Emmaus road, the way of the attentive ear and ready availability.

This kind of nun is committed to the coming of the Kingdom or reign of God, to the transformation of society and its structures, to working in a world that feels neither brave nor new. She works in the shanty towns of the poor, in hospices for the terminally sick, anywhere where the marginalized and the weak are made welcome. But she is also there in the lecture theatres of universities, in the houses of the great, in the corridors of power. This stirs mixed reactions in a number of people. They wonder if it is appropriate work for someone who ought to be all good and humble. And this is an indication of how deeply the rot has set in. We have a great deal of trouble with the image of the professional adult Christian woman and apparently none at all with the professional adult Christian man. Moreover, where there has been some movement on this question, the presence of nuns has often been unhelpful. In parishes where women are asked to be ministers of the Eucharist, priests have often selected the women religious before or in preference to the married or single women of the parish. This does not make sense, even as a ploy to enable women to approach the altar. Any woman, any person, can be chosen for this task; why create élites?

The professional nun can be parodied, too. Where I work we receive a magazine which is circulated free to all offices in central London. On the singing telegram adverts page, I read that the following services are available: kissagrams and strippagrams. These include stripping nuns, stripping nurses, stripping traffic wardens and policewomen. This publication is in no way deliberately pornographic, so that more extreme or more salacious delights must be left to the imagination. My point is that nuns, nurses, traffic wardens and policewomen, let alone women lawyers and women politicians – any professional women, in fact – are assumed to be acting out of role and therefore to be good for a laugh. The fact that they may put on uniform is seen not as something functional but as a statement of intent for which they should be humiliated. The sexual overtones are not incidental; the implication is that every woman should be getting it somewhere, and the fellows, therefore, are free to fantasize about giving it.

Yet the teaching sister and the nursing sister and the sister who spends her morning in the juvenile courts and her afternoon in the cells is taking Christ with her in a very explicit way. She is a woman with whom all women can identify because the image she projects is of Christ present in the world, an engaged, intervening Christ whose reign is stirring in the world, an engaged, intervening Christ whose reign is stirring in our midst. She is a parable of the condition of us all. The apostolic religious sister is only 'different' in that her vows of chastity, poverty and obedience dedicate her formally to discipleship in a way which is beholden on everyone. She is consecrated or committed by vow, just as a married person is consecrated or committed by vow. For this reason, what is true of her has some general validity; her experience speaks to the experience of many women in the Church. In their own sphere of competence they are experienced professional people, faced with decisions that affect people and situations. Both the positive and negative aspects of this experience will ring bells with anyone who has tried to open her mouth at a parish council meeting, has refused the popular image of the docile, acquiescent person-in-the-benches, has felt and acted out of principle notably in the area of her own sexuality and sexual responsibility. The call to be adult and woman, when coupled with the advantages of professional formation, can lead to a variety of responses, and the Church needs them all.

The radical nun

The idea of a radical nun, meanwhile, might seem somewhat overwhelming. Yet those who founded most religious Orders, when they first set out were very radical women, women who were prepared to look at the roots of their own and the world's motivation and do something about them. I am particularly aware of Mary Ward in this context because she was the first foundress of a consciously active apostolic religious Order, and was quite clear that, in her own words, 'women, in time to come, will be seen to do much'. Radical nuns nowadays are there on the barbed-wire fences at Greenham Common, they are familiar faces to the police who monitor civil rights and anti-nuclear marches. They are known to the police in other ways, too, because they provide safe houses for victims of violence, for the battered and the homeless. They are not afraid to be on the fringes of convention, because they see the gospel as a challenge that ought to transform our every perception and relationship. They seek to live the gospel naked, as it were, and not at one remove from behind the security of established convention, even established religious convention. There are radical nuns among the ranks of the real nuns and of the apostolic sisters as well, just as there are radical women among the housewives and the professional women.

91

Like all radical women they are open to parody, and the appearance of a book like *Breaking Silence* (with its subtitle 'Lesbian Nuns on Convent Sexuality') does little to dispel this image. 'Radical' and 'misfit' are words we are inclined to couple together without serious reflection; we misread the signs or read them through middle-class eyes. Yet the dirty-jeans nun or the feminist-slogan nun is one a lot of people find hard to handle. And the pun is deliberate, because my intimation is that behind the image we fear some kind of denial of sexuality. Why should this be the case? Why do we imagine that there is something unfeminine about jeans and not about the full habit with all its flattening propensities? I have worn both and know how easy it is to hide behind the habit, to hide both from myself and from other people. Nuns, like married and single people, are called to be whole women; all that is different is that we come to completion through vowed celibacy rather than through marriage, childbirth and other forms of chastity.

Once again these observations have a general application. The Church really does have a difficulty with the single woman, unless she is a nun, because her way of coming to God falls outside the norm established by a religion that appears to value the married state to the exclusion of almost everything else. Single women may not wish to be identified with the radical nuns, many married people may feel that the way in which they live is radical. My point is that the Church often pushes unmarried women to the fringes because it fails to appreciate that theirs is a valid option. Celibacy does not have to be vowed to be valid. There are alternatives, there are a variety of different ways of answering God's call; the choice is not simply between the married state and the religious life. The choice is not simply to be defined in terms of the relationship one has with men. For this reason the feminist graffiti which reads, 'Feel superior; become a nun' may be misguided in its assumption that we are again talking about superiority and inferiority, but it is accurate in allying nuns with the cause.

What matters is that we be clear about the alternatives, about the self-understanding of reflective women, whether married, single or religious. Women religious are people who seek to make sense of chastity and poverty and obedience in a world in which it is hard to love with all one is and has and does. Their vows are no more mysterious than that. For this reason the Second Vatican

Council reminded Roman Catholics that a degree of chastity, poverty and obedience is beholden upon each one of us. Where God empowers a person to live totally out of this understanding, we are given a parable to help us spin our own story more convincingly. Where God empowers a person to live alone or to build the Kingdom within marriage we are given other parables, each of which is equally valid, from each of which we can learn. I can hear these lessons when a friend writes,

> My brother and his wife now have a beautiful son called Eric who is my first nephew. Did you know that? I'm all mixed up. Immediately wanted to have a baby. Down hormones, down. There's a thing in *Lear* about knocking the buggers on the head. Imagine them as eels slithering out of a mixing bowl, and being knocked on the head with a pestle by a big fat woman in a calico apron. Being a woman is so dangerous . . .
>
> Louisa Blair, Ignatius Farm Community,
> Guelph, Ontario, 25 July 1987

Vowed religious are increasingly learning from other women that chastity and poverty and obedience commit us to relate to the world in new ways and that these ways are not safe; they are dangerous because costly. An understanding of the religious life which is formed by images of renunciation (of sex, money and power for instance) forces people to retreat from God's call rather than to answer it. Vowed chastity is about a commitment to enter into non-oppressive, non-possessive relationships with named people; vowed poverty is being seen much more in terms of a commitment to share what one has and what one is given; vowed obedience as a commitment to seek God's will at all times. Each is costly because discipleship and all growth into freedom are costly – and nuns do not have a monopoly on this understanding.

Women as Church in the world

The inferences for ministry – what this means for women who are the Church in the world – are significant. Ministry is not the preserve of any one group in the Church. It is available to all once they have the confidence to take themselves seriously and to open up to God's vocation. Far too many women have been unable to say the words 'I have a vocation' because this phrase has been given such a limited application and meaning. Each Christian vocation has been impoverished and so, too, has each Christian response to this vocation. The God who calls and the God who empowers our response is one and the same God. Right now I want to call her God the kangaroo. Jesus was content to compare himself to a hen (Matt. 23.37; Luke 13.34), the Scriptures speak of a God who raises us up on eagle's wings (Exod. 19.4) or is a bear (Lam. 3.10), so I have no problem with this animal image. A kangaroo is an unusual mother because she gives birth twice. At the first the little roo is embryonic. She emerges from the birth passage onto a pathway her mother has licked smooth for her and which leads to the pouch. Into this she scrambles and completes her gestation, emerging only when she is ready because the mother feeds her inside the pouch. God lets us be born slowly, emerging one process at a time, she too feeds us and helps us grow, enfolding and sheltering us without in any way letting us become or remain infantile.

> God, I like it when you hop about
> It's full of unexpected and delight
> And here I am sharing your view
> Your way of looking at the story and the people and the world.
>
> When first I was born I clung to the slippery
> slope and did not realize that you had
> prepared a path for me
> Now I'm in your pouch it's like being in
> your handbag – that safe, that chaotic, that arbitrary,
> that needed.
>
> And so I can pray:
> Mother there and Mother here
> I am with you
> Touch me　　　Change me
> Feed me　　　Forgive me
> Teach me　　　Protect me
> Hold me　　　Enfold me
> And throw me out,
> to hop about your world, Amen

To minister to the world from within the safety of God's handbag is not a way we ordinarily see our task in life. The occasional fresh insight such as this does not harm, however, and can remind us of something we already know – that our presence in the world does make a difference to how God is able to organize herself. It certainly demythologizes some of our grander notions of ministry or apostolic purpose, and may give a hint about where to begin.

What I am suggesting is this: the kind of reflective living in the world envisaged by the integrating spirituality described here will necessarily lead us to seek a faith-filled life in service of the world. Women who live present to God in certain ways within the world will want to share this vision with others. Essentially ours will be an apostolic spirituality, and yet this word 'apostolic' requires some explanation. We have been led to think that apostles are the twelve named in the Gospels and therefore that to be an apostle one has first to be a man. In reality, apostles are people who are freed by Jesus and sent by Jesus as witnesses to his resurrection. We are freed from excessive preoccupation with ourselves, from fear and from meaninglessness. But we are also freed *for*, liberated so that we can serve. Teresa of Avila wrote, 'Christ has no other hands on earth but yours.' Women who are freed for service, enabled by God to be people for others, see ministry as a way of relating to other people, a way to living in the world as believing people. Our hands are Christ's hands in the world. Our experience of the baptismal call and consecration to holiness is increasingly finding form and expression in everything we do. Our experience is that we are apostolic women.

From its earliest days the Church has admitted that the active apostolic response is one it treasures. In the Acts of the Apostles there are people who minister to the word and people who minister directly to the church community; people who preach and people who offer hospitality. The tradition is crowded out with instances of ways in which the Churches have sought to organize this ministry, better to centre it on real people and their needs, better to make it serve the interests of the Kingdom. These are to be understood as insights into the value of an apostolic response to God's call rather than constraining ways in which to read and evaluate present-day answers to that call. Christian truth will always be different to other truth because its perspective is the future, the coming age, rather than the past and what worked then. God who is in the midst of us does more than knock us on the head with a pestle. Her calico apron is servicable and serves to shelter the world. She wears it with the tenacity and courage with which she fills her handbag.

For this reason, those who feel called to reclaim ministry and to be apostles in today's Church are becoming increasingly inventive and creative in their response to this call. The fields are ripe for harvest as never before; the world so evidently needs people whose sense of vocation is going to lead them to seek and find God in the real, the professional and the radical. Above all, however, the Church needs women to diversify and extend the place and purpose of apostolic presence in the world.

8
On being Woman
in the Church

∽

Women in the Church

If thinking about ministry in general leads to insights into the place
of women in the world, the question of ordination centres much
more specifically on the place of women within the faith community of the local, national or international Church. In those
Churches that do not ordain women we nevertheless have an
instant congregation in the form of the parish or faith community
of our own home and family. My intention in this final chapter is to
look at the way in which women in particular can minister to the
formation of those with whom we form faith community. In time,
what we do within the domestic Church will have a more general
application because it cannot be long before the fundamentalist
reasoning behind many attempts to refuse ordination to women in
certain other Churches are recognized for what they are – instances
of injustice rather than anything else.

This fundamentalism was well observed in a letter written to
The Tablet in the light of a recent proscription from Rome: women,
we have been told, are not to have their feet washed at Maundy
Thursday celebrations because women did not have their feet
washed by Jesus at the final supper he shared with his friends. The
letter read:

> Cardinal Mayer, in his support for the Bishop of Pittsburgh,
> does not go far enough. He excludes women from the washing
> of feet in the liturgy of Holy Thursday because Christ washed
> the feet only of males. The argument against the ordaining of
> women is that Christ ordained only men. Let us, please, take
> these arguments to their logical conclusion. Let us exclude

women from the Eucharist since at the last supper Christ shared
his body and blood only with men.

Letter from Catherine Ivinson of Florida, USA,
The Tablet, 10 May 1986

While Rome fiddles and tinkers, the world burns. And sadly,
other Christians who have already ordained women within their
communions are tempted to join the fiddling and shop women in
the name of some greater apparent good, for instance Christian
unity. In a sense, though, this is a separate debate and one that will
be quickly overtaken by events.

Images of priesthood

If the presence of women among the ranks of the ordained is to
make a significant difference, this time of waiting can be used to
explore what we already contribute and the ways in which we are
already exercising the priesthood which is ours by right in virtue of
our baptism. Women as priests are people whose identity and
experience is such that the public expression of what we do within
the community of believers is about service rather than servitude.
On a recent visit to Toronto I was struck by the ease and friendli-
ness with which people served me in shops and coffee bars. They
did not find this service demeaning, and so did not resent giving it.
In England we seem reluctant to serve each other and the gospel
image of service suffers in consequence. Yet Jesus was content to
serve; we are called to freedom not to slavery. God the liberator
sets us free from false images of Christian service. But, as is the
case with all the false securities we use to cocoon ourselves, these
can only be abandoned when we know what they are, where they
come from, and when we see where they are taking us.

Amongst such images is the understanding that God has
somehow to be placated and therefore that Christian service is a
bloody affair. God is a tyrant who demands propitiation, a fickle,
elusive being who is always calling us to make efforts beyond our
capacity. I heard him described recently as God the lumberjack
who calls us through a deserted landscape populated by only the
felled trees and ashes of our life and aspirations. His priest presides
at this holocaust, calling for more victims, more sacrifice. The altar
overshadows the table as the central place of Christian meeting,
and Communion becomes a sharing in pain rather than each other.

Another image of God which leads to a distorted perception of Christian service is that of God as judge. The judge is never off duty; his priest, too, is endlessly on the look-out, endlessly concerned to bring people to repentance. The sin of which we are to repent is not our involvement in a world and a political framework that denies human rights, lets half the world starve while the other half stockpiles weapons of hideous strength and sells weak people to the strong. The sin in question is rather our own personal worthlessness, our tendency to fail, our very humanity. This priest sends people down spirals of guilt with the ease with which one creates a centrifugal force by pulling out a bath-plug. Yet he inevitably has his eyes closed to issues of justice. He is the priest Jeremiah castigated, the one who cannot see the connection between love of God and love of neighbour. His only concern is to make people realize that God has judged them and found them wanting. Liturgical celebration resonates to the cries of thunder and violence, the table becomes a board to thump and Communion a luxury.

God can be imaged as a bodiless spirit, too, so that his priest is one whose only concern is with the soul and with the quest for higher thought. He is certainly not interested in our anxieties about money and sex and food, or in our desire to make sense of the world in which we live. He cannot serve our basic needs because these are not deemed to exist. Where the 'spiritual life' is set up in opposition to the rest of life, strange things begin to happen. We can all think of instances when we have been led to hide from our own experience, when Sunday has been hived off from the rest of the week, the sanctuary from the world and vice versa. The Lord's table becomes a refuge from reality, Communion a travesty of Jesus' words about taking and eating his body. I cannot help but notice that it is Julian of Norwich who enables me to hit that idea on the head when she writes, 'Our sensuality is founded in nature, in mercy and in grace, and this foundation enables us to receive gifts which lead us to endless life' (*Showings*, Long text, ch. 55).

Each of these false images of Christian priesthood is based on an equally false image of God and, in turn, it generates an equally false image of Christian living. For this reason, because these images are so strong and their influence so pervasive, it is useful to understand the mechanism whereby we create them. Otherwise where they are not admitted we assume that we are acting out of principle, and can end up confusing taste with truth.

If the great Christian commandment is to love, the great Christian temptation must be to fear. We fall into fear or envy or pride because we fail to take our baptism seriously. By baptism into the Christian community we are bound to each other in bonds of trust, committed to journeying towards God in a way that precludes hostility and jealousy. Most people live as pagans, in the sense of unbaptized people, for long years after they first receive the sacrament. Appropriating one's baptism takes time. Appropriating one's humanity takes time. Learning to live as a human being and member of the human community is not easy. The local faith community of the family is the first place where we start this learning and where our images are first formed. And so I ask in what ways women work there. In any human group what is the place of women? My own experience is that they are people who have listened to me and fed me, they are people with whom I have been free to be vulnerable and free to ask questions. They have not overwhelmed me with the power and significance of their own ideas but have encouraged me to think my own thoughts and to be serious about living in terms of what I have discovered to be true. They have encouraged me when I was depressed and supported me when I was using my gifts and talents.

In contrast, holy mother Church – and each denomination has one – has not always named God particularly helpfully or enabled me to grow to adult status as a believer. In its anxiety to help me identify myself as Christian, the official teaching Church has sometimes spoken of faith as though it were the same as certainty. Yet as an adult, growing, believing person I am always learning to name God more closely and with more love. And if the Church were a real mother instead of a pretend one she would know that faith will inevitably be mixed with doubt, that the experience of believing will often feel like the experience of doubting. Dark nights of faith and clouds of unknowing are part of the Christian vocabulary, so why do I have to wait to be an adult to discover this? The experience of growing to God may be a painful one but it is made doubly so where the Church appears to desire no more than my notional assent.

Faith that is learnt in the home and the family of the Church should image God in ways which demonstrate that development is of the nature of belief. I have suggested that three unhelpful images of God can throw up three equally unhelpful images of priesthood and of Christian living. By starting from the position of the people from whom we learn our images in the first instance, namely women in the home, we could see ways in which a further image may be supplied, one that is informed by this experience.

For this reason I believe it is useful to explore certain understandings that result if one were to take further the premises with which I have been working in this book. The first is that both men and women can know God; the second is that God is neither male nor female because God is mystery. The human language we use to talk about God, like the human language that Jesus used, is always analogous; that is to say God is father and mother and friend and lover and air and fire and wind and earthquake and a host of other things besides. Each of these is only one word, only one human way of trying to say something about the mystery. None is absolute; none can ever make a definitive statement about the nature and purpose and intentions of God. Each is an indication of our conviction that God does wish to be known.

Where Jesus called God 'Father', he was identifying God in terms of a relationship and, in the same breath, defining himself as son. If relationships are that central, they must be the cradle out of which our understanding of Christian life and service can grow. The woman priest whose personal faith has been nurtured within a faith community or family where her experience of relationships has been sound is obviously in a strong position to name other relationships in ways that are sound. This business of naming is not a way of saying that the priest's task is simply to teach. Rather, I have suggested that it lies at the heart of sacramental ministry as well. The woman who creates community in the home and from whom her children learn both how to grow *into* the family and how to grow *away* from the family towards other people gives us an image of God who wills that we come to human maturity. The woman who gathers friends around her table to celebrate their relationships and the human events of their lives gives us an image of God who wills that we take each other and our everyday human experience seriously. The woman who listens and who cleans and who cares for the people in her home gives us the image of a God who is concerned with the physical, a God who really will raise us up body and soul as whole people. Again I am not surprised when I find this insight endorsed by Julian of Norwich. 'For I saw very surely that our substance is in God, and I also saw that God is our sensuality, for in that same instant and place in which our soul is made sensual, in that same instant and place exists the city of God, ordained by him from without beginning' (*Showings* Long text, ch. 55). The woman who goes out to work, whether in factory or school or law courts or operating theatre, is taking with her an interiorized understanding of community, and reminding us that God is at work and at play in our world and in all our human groups.

Where the Church ignores this rich tradition of community-making, images of priesthood as well as of God necessarily suffer. Where this tradition is allowed to speak to our present-day needs, it can counteract the temptation we have to image God as tyrant, judge or bodiless spirit. It can counteract the tendency we have to make a mockery of priesthood in tying it to the placation of such a God. In their place we have imaged in women's presence in the Church a God who nurtures and empowers, a God who is both life and love. The image of priesthood that is generated from this understanding is of the priest who in turn is called to nurture and to empower; to be both life and love.

The priest who nurtures

While a new image of sacramental practice does well to build upon whatever is best in the old, images of feeding are complicated because food has, at times, been withheld from believing Christians as though we were naughty children. The Jesus who said 'Take and eat' (Matt. 26.26) has had his words hedged about with man-made rules and regulations. Or, there again, food has been identified too narrowly with certain activities – called sacraments – and not with others. The power of this image is diminished when it is treated as part of a punishment or rewards system. Nevertheless some of our sacramental imagery can be retrieved from a tradition that has seen sacraments as ways in which God's life can be shared by God's community, where the emphasis has been on the process of feeding rather than upon the notion of food; on life as sacrament rather than upon sacraments as the only form of life.

The task of feeding people is one that requires dedication, creativity, knowledge. Above all it requires commitment to the growing process, to the notion that what one is doing is nurturing independent life. When the adult of any species is enabled to stand independently from its parents, then has the task of nurturing been achieved. Where nurturing is used to increase dependence and to destroy the growing person's selfhood, then nurturing becomes a travesty of itself and an image of abnegation. One of the most powerful of eucharistic images we hold from the tradition is that of the pelican. He does not merely feed his young but is ready to destroy himself in the process. If God is imaged as nurturer, then the image is of the nurturer for whom no sacrifice is excessive. Feeding is all, because feeding is about the development of other people.

In this sense the challenge for the priesthood nowadays is to find ways of nurturing that are compatible with the insight that Christians are called to adult life in the faith community. The patriarch, the head of the village community, the devoted pastor of the flock, have to give way to images of a nurturing presence that takes human development seriously. 'When the big bang comes on Monday,' I heard a city priest say recently, apropos of the reorganization of London's Stock Exchange, 'I hope that people in the business world know that they can count on the support of their priest in the ensuing stress.' How, I could not help wondering, are they to know that this is the case? Clerical presence is often so static, so tied to certain premisses and not to others, to certain practices and not to others, that how are the generality of nominal or otherwise Christians to know that the Church has any interest at all in what is of real concern to them? I am not arguing for more sacraments here; sacraments for the big bang, for visiting the doctor, for hitting forty or whatever. All that I am suggesting is that there are levels of belief that may require different models of practice and of celebration. At different stages in anyone's faith journey different ways of meeting the individual believer's spiritual needs have to be envisaged. A nurturing model of forming people as believers is one that takes these needs seriously because it enables one to separate the feeding from the food. In the past we often gave people sacraments and thought we were nurturing their faith. Nowadays that equation cannot be made and so the function of priests has to be envisaged differently.

Faith formation has to be taken out of the church building and taken back to the place where the rest of our formation happens: the home, the street, the pub and the park. In these places the ministry of women has always been important and our specific role in the formation process recognized. The actual quality of what we accomplish there has to be examined without sentiment, however; otherwise one is back into false images of Christian presence. It is not because we are gentle and loving and long-suffering that our presence is to be valued. We do not represent the triumph of *anima* over *animus*.

The quality of this presence has more to do with the fact that our model of engagement is a nurturing one. For cultural reasons we have been able both to own and to share what we are feeling and so have not been forced to act inhumanly. The tradition of interdependent relationships, of friendship and co-operation, is ours by right. The communities of women to which I have belonged have been places where the ability to relate to people has been prized above all else, where a sense of humour is considered essential if one is to grow and to enjoy life, where false piety has been given very short shrift. They have been formation communities in the best sense of the word, and places where the Church has had its greatest influence on me.

The God who empowers

Yet God is more than a God who creates us, God is a God who redeems us, too. The God who is engaged in the human story gives life, certainly, but also loves us through into the abundance of life we call the Kingdom. Priests of this God empower others. In practice, this means that those whom the Churches ordain to serve the needs of the believing community are committed to certain attitudes which, of their very nature, seek to give power away rather than to hoard it.

Initially this means sharing knowledge. Information about the Churches, hard factual information about finances and distribution of personnel, is hard to come by. Further education and theological literacy are only now becoming available in any general sense. Is the God imaged one who seeks to share the divine life with us or a God who has secrets? The degree of openness displayed by those whose function it is to minister to the community of believers says a great deal about their understanding of God. Where people cling to their learning they are clinging to power at the expense of others; where they share information and knowledge they empower others and set them free. What they do

104

with their power can never be neutral. In the same way the language of sharing has to be a language that demystifies rather than a jargon that encodes. Sharing means listening to the language used by the other in order to speak back in words that sound accessible and familiar. Sharing such as this means speaking in lay language.

Additionally, those who are priests can no longer hide behind archaic images of what it is to be a committed Christian. A human priesthood is committed to being a humane priesthood. Anything which demythologizes the pagan understanding behind the formation and maintenance of a priestly caste can be dropped in favour of gospel presence. The quality of lay presence in the world, of women's presence in the world, is one that can do much to restore an understanding of gospel presence within the Church.

Recently I was asked to talk to a group of young men who were preparing for the sacrament of orders. They came from four continents and represented the pick of their generation. I asked them to reflect on and to identify the qualities they most admired in the people they were conscious of as they prepared for ordination. Each of them admired things such as availability, a commitment to personal prayer, a sense of service and so on. Each of them named another priest as the person who most clearly exemplified these qualities. When I suggested that they then reflect back to me some of the qualities they most admired in their parents, we had a totally unexpected conversation about the place of their mothers and sisters in their development as believing people, and about women in general.

Later this led me to ask myself further questions about the exact way in which the leaven transforms the lump. It is as easy to be sentimental about the laity in general as it is about women in particular. Essentially lay presence is about people rather than structures and institutions; essentially lay presence is about seeking and finding a God who lives within; essentially lay presence is about valuing all the ways in which we journey to God rather than only some of them. Lay people have ordinarily had to face up to the reality of how their sexual responses form part of their faith response more realistically than most clerics – even non-celibate clerics. Lay people have not been able to hide from the need to work out how money should be used as a Kingdom value, or where they stand on political and social issues as easily as most of those whom the Churches presently ordain. Lay people, in general, know what it means to live by the sweat of one's brow. The God who empowers their faith response is God the redeemer of relationships, of sex, money, work, of pleasure and pain, of a Kingdom which is in the midst of us. This God is given to us in the vision all Christians share in common, the vision of Jesus who calls us to share in all the mysteries of his life, death and resurrection. The Christbearer, whether lay or ordained, is the one who can say 'I am baptized, I am transfigured, I am taken, blessed, broken and given and, ultimately, I have died with Christ and am risen with him, I appear on the Emmaus road and share the Christian story with others.' The Christian mysteries are lived out again in the individual woman's or man's experience of growing to God.

Where women empower others by sharing this knowledge with them and by engaging in the real practical events of day-to-day living with those with whom we live or work, where women priests in particular minister to the growing life of a Kingdom which is within the world of the known and the familiar, then God is imaged as liberator, as the one who transforms our world and our power structures. For this reason alone a whole priesthood, where named people minister to the life of the community from below rather than from above, is more than one very viable pattern for the future, it is the only way forward.

The model of priesthood that emerges is of priest as servant or deacon to the deep needs of the Christian community, to the need we all have to make sense of our world and our lives in Christian terms. Moreover it leaves me with questions. Does one have to be ordained to answer this calling? Does one have to be ordained for ever? Who does the ordaining: someone from above or the group which is going to be served by the minister in question? These are questions I could not have envisaged myself ever asking in the Birmingham Oratory of my childhood. The Roman Catholic world I looked out onto then seemed set fair to last for ever. It was a world where everyone had a place. Mine was definitely marked out for me in the brass nameplate on the bench in front of me as I gazed with attentive concentration at the back of the priest celebrating amid clouds of incense in the sanctuary. I should have been more attentive to the significance of the fact that the incense made my mother cough and that she led the family in prayer at home. I should have listened to the Bible stories my grandmother taught me – about the importance of tides in the Red Sea and flights of quails from northern Europe. Instead I had to wait until the Second Vatican Council and for permission to start thinking things through in terms of the known and the familiar, in terms, in fact, of the world made by the women – and men – who first formed me.

Role models for women priests

One final question which relates to the present. I asked the wife of a bishop who has been ordaining women for ten years what role models she imagined were available to the women priests of her husband's diocese. Her first answer was 'Jesus'. When pressed, she claimed that there are a number of older men whom any young woman could look up to and admire. Neither answer seems totally satisfactory. The first because it is an inadequate description of Christian discipleship; the second because once again it fails to honour the idea that something new is happening in Churches that do choose to ordain women. Something more useful is being said when women are freed to choose other women as role models. In this instance in particular, that lay women should be role models for women priests, rather than the other way round, gives rise to new ways of celebrating and of ministering with which to transform clerical structures and practice.

I am also conscious that most religious communities are communities of women. When we wish to celebrate the Eucharist we have to import a male chaplain to preside at the centre of our liturgical life. In communities where male priests are unable to come and officiate for us, new forms of celebration and, more importantly, new styles of presiding are being developed. These demonstrate that in the eucharistic context, too, there are role models to be examined and followed. The experience of many groups of women, as well as of individual women, is reflected in a friend's comment on what happens in her community when the priest oversleeps. 'We have our own Eucharist and have found that the rite for celebrating with the sick is the one that best meets our needs; you see, there is no president in that and so we can just sit round and take it in turns.'

If I return to the words Mary Ward wrote in 1615, 'And it will be seen that women in time to come will do much,' it is because I believe that we are living in the time she spoke of, that this is the day of salvation. Increasingly, as I speak with and listen to people, women and men, religious and ordained, Roman Catholics and Anglicans, people from the Free Churches as well as people from no named Church at all, I am conscious that we are witnessing the kind of groundswell of popular feeling that is the mark of the Spirit's presence and activity in the world. The Spirit who brooded over the first creation and who now broods over her new creation reminds us that we are at present living with chaos. The waters are not untroubled, but a new way is clear where it is recognized that 'male and female God made them. In God's own image they are made' (Gen. 1.27). We are called to the glory of finding God's image within and of enabling others to recognize their own glory, too.

To return to my own beginnings: I choose to end with the experience of Thérèse of Lisieux who wrote from the heart of French nineteenth-century ghetto Catholicism:

> To be betrothed to you, Jesus, to be a Carmelite, to become, through my union with you, a mother of souls – surely that ought to be enough for anybody? But somehow, not for me. I seem to have so many other vocations as well! I feel as if I were called to be a fighter, a priest, an apostle, a doctor, a martyr . . . I want to be a priest.

(*Autobiography of a Saint*
tr. Ronald Knox (Fontana 1960), pp. 183–4)

She died at the age of twenty-four and herself observed that this was the age at which, in other circumstances, she would have been ordained. There are other women with the same desires, the same sense of vocation; women who are instances and places of where the city of God is. What will the Churches do about this?

Bibliography

⁓

Works cited in the text

p.14 Charlesworth, James H., ed. and tr., *The Odes of Solomon* (Scholars Press 1977), Ode 19, pp.82-3.

pp.14, 99, 102 *Showings*, Long text, tr. Edmund Colledge OSA and James Walsh SJ. The Classics of Western Spirituality, SPCK 1978.

p.15 The Mary Ward quotation is taken from *Till God Will* ed. M. Emmanuel Orchard IBVM (Darton, Longman and Todd), p.9.

p.64 Fowler, James W., *Stages of Faith*. San Francisco, Harper and Row, 1981.

p.92 Curb, Rosemary, and Manahan, Nancy, *Breaking Silence: Lesbian Nuns on Convent Sexuality*. Columbus Books 1985.

Biblical

Brown, Raymond, *Biblical Reflections on Crises facing the Church* (Mahwah, NJ, Paulist Press, 1975).

Fiorenza, Elisabeth Schüssler, *In Memory of Her: A Feminist Reconstruction of Christian Origins* (SCM Press 1983).

Perkins, Pheme, *Ministers in the Pauline Churches* (Mahwah, NJ, Paulist Press, 1982).

Russell, Letty (ed.), *Feminist Interpretation of the Bible* (Basil Blackwell 1985).

Schneiders, Sandra, *Women and the Word: The Gender of God in the New Testament and the Spirituality of Women* (Mahwah, NJ, Paulist Press, 1986).

Tetlow, Elizabeth, *Women and Ministry in the New Testament* (Mahwah, NJ, Paulist Press, 1980).

General Theology

Ashe, Kaye, *Today's Woman, Tomorrow's Church* (Chicago, Thomas More Press, 1983).

Daly, Mary, *The Church and the Second Sex* (Geoffrey Chapman 1968).

Fiorenza, Elisabeth Schüssler and Collins, Mary (eds.), *Women: Invisible in Church and Theology* (Concilium, 182, December 1985, T. & T. Clark).

Kroll, Una, *Flesh of my Flesh* (Darton, Longman and Todd 1975).

Maitland, Sara, *A Map of the New Country: Women and Christianity* (Routledge and Kegan Paul 1983).

Moltmann-Wendel, Elisabeth, *A Land Flowing with Milk and Honey* (SCM Press 1986).

Moltmann-Wendel, Elisabeth and Moltmann, Jurgen, *Humanity in God* (Routledge and Kegan Paul 1983).

Ruether, Rosemary Radford, *Mary: The Feminine Face of the Church* (SCM Press 1979).

Ruether, Rosemary Radford, *Sexism and God-Talk* (SCM Press 1983).

Ruether, Rosemary Radford, *To Change the World: Christology and Cultural Criticism* (SCM Press 1981).

Ruether, Rosemary Radford, *Womanguides: Readings towards a Feminist Theology* (Boston, Beacon Press, 1985).

Russell, Letty, *Human Liberation in a Feminist Perspective – a Theology* (Philadelphia, Westminister Press, 1974).

Soelle, Dorothee, *Choosing Life* (SCM Press 1981).

Soelle, Dorothee, *The Strength of the Weak: Towards a Christian Feminist Identity* (Philadelphia, Westminister Press, 1984).

Ministry

Chittister, Joan; *Winds of Change: Women Challenge the Church* (Sheed and Ward 1986).

Chittister, Joan, *Women, Ministry and the Church* (Mahwah, NJ, Paulist Press, 1983).

Furlong, Monica, *Feminine in the Church* (SPCK 1984).

Mary Ward: Journey into Freedom (Way Supplement 53, Way Publications).

Woman (*The Way*, vol. 26, April 1986, Way Publications).

Bynum, Caroline Walker, *Jesus as Mother: Studies in the Spirituality of the Middle Ages* (University of California Press 1982).

Clark, Elizabeth, *Women in the Early Church* (Wilmington, DE, Michael Glazier, 1967).

Dronke, Peter, *Women Writers in the Middle Ages* (Cambridge University Press 1984).

Nicholas, Joanna and Shark, Lillian Thomas, *Distant Echoes: Medieval Religious Women, I* (Kalamazoo, Cistercian Publications, 1984).

Weaver, Mary Jo, *New Catholic Women* (Harper and Row 1986).

Spirituality

Garcia, Jo and Maitland, Sara (eds.), *Walking on the Water: Women Talk about Spirituality* (Virago Press 1983).

Giles, Mary (ed.), *The Feminist Mystic and other Essays on Women and Spirituality* (New York, Crossroads, 1982).

King, Ursula, *Voices of Protest: Voices of Promise Exploring Spirituality for a New Age* (The Hibbert Trust 1984).

Osiek, Carolyn, *Beyond Anger: On being a Feminist in the Church* (Mahwah, NJ. Paulist Press, 1986).

Wolski Conn, Joanna, *Women's Spirituality: Resources for Christian Deveplopment* (Mahwah, NJ, Paulist Press, 1986).

Women for what World? In what Church? (*Donum Dei*, 30, 1985 Canadian Religious Conference).